Encounter Jesus in the Gospels and Daily Life

Encountering Jesus in the Gospels and Daily Life

RONALD LEINEN, MSC

Canticle Books

A Publication of Magnus Press

Canticle Books

A Publication of Magnus Press
P.O. Box 2666
Carlsbad, CA 92018

Encountering Jesus in the Gospels and Daily Life

All rights reserved. No part of this book may be reproduced in any form without permission from the publisher.

First Edition, 2000

Printed in the United States of America

Publisher's Cataloguing-in-Publication
(Provided by Quality Books, Inc.)

Leinen, Ronald.
    Encountering Jesus in the gospels and daily life/
Ronald Leinen. -- 1st ed.
    p. cm.
    LCCN: 00-107826
    ISBN: 0-9654806-7-4
    1. Jesus Christ--Example--Bible teaching.
2. Christian life--Anecdotes. 3. Biible. N.T. Gospels--
Criticism, interpretation, etc.   I. Title

BT304.2.L45 2000   232.9'04
                     QBI00-806

TABLE OF CONTENTS

INTRODUCTION

In my personal search for Jesus, I have sought the one of whom I have learned from Christians who have gone before me. They have left me their impressions in the Bible and in the traditions which have been handed down through 2000 years. Jesus' Church has refined our understanding of him. Nevertheless, I must still search for him in my heart as I pray and try to live a Christian life. Though from the beginning of my search I needed to understand that the Gospels are the revealed word of God about Jesus, greater than all personal thoughts and feelings, I still needed to discover Jesus in my life experience if I was to undergo a change of heart..

My search began in my early twenties, when after years of spiritual drifting I rediscovered Jesus as a lover and savior. The rediscovery also profoundly changed my life. In the Song of Solomon, the lover sings:

I opened to my beloved,
> but my beloved had turned
> and was gone.
My soul failed me when he spoke.
> I sought him but did not find him;
> I called him, but he gave no answer....

The chorus responds:

Where has your beloved gone,
> O fairest among women?
Which way has your beloved turned,
> that we may seek him with you? (Song 5:6, 6:1)

The Jesus whom I sought then and seek now is the one who touched the lives and hearts of people in the Gospels and who lives today. I find him, then and now, proclaiming the good news to all the world but especially the poor of this world, for Jesus was first and foremost a missionary sent by his Father.

I find him too in his ongoing healing of the spirits, minds and bodies of those whom I have come to know over the years, and in my own life. I will tell some of my own story and the stories of others in whom I have seen the loving work of Jesus. To protect their identities, when they are not already well known, I shall not use their real names.

Throughout my career as a seminarian and a priest, I have been convinced that the answer people give to the question "Who is Jesus?" is critical for their spiritual lives. It is my hope that this book will be of service in making Jesus better known, as he is presented in the Gospels and in the way he reaches out with compassion and love in the lives of people today.

In regard to the Gospel portrayal of Jesus, this book is not a scholarly study of Scripture. The four evangelists each had specific purposes in shaping their message. They were proclaiming the good news to different people with particular needs. It is the scholar's task to try to discern the setting and purpose of each evangelist. This book seeks to provide a living experience of Jesus from many perspectives. The mystery of Jesus is larger than any one of them.

Each chapter concludes with a prayer. Meditating on the Gospels is our main source of knowledge about Jesus, and the book begins on gospel themes and related reflections. Yet, like the first disciples, we need to discover Jesus in daily life before we can give ourselves over to Jesus' love and share in his mission. Therefore, the second half of the book tries to learn about Jesus from what he is doing in the lives of people in our day. Let us then begin our journey to discover "Who is Jesus?" and encounter him anew.

PART I: JESUS IN THE GOSPELS

Chapter 1: LET ME SEE AGAIN

We begin our search for a deeper knowledge of Jesus by coming upon him in the middle of his ministry in ancient Israel. The advantage of beginning there is that we can see the humanness and compassion of the Lord reaching out to the poorest and the most despised of his brothers and sisters. This was a central feature of his life and work among us, from its beginning to its conclusion. It illuminates both his origins and his destiny.

We meet him on a personal level, much closer to our daily lives than the Jesus of theology or history. We come to know him intimately—heart speaking to heart. Mark relates just such a story of a blind man who met Jesus (10:46-52): "They came to Jericho. As he and his disciples and a large crowd were leaving Jericho, Bartimaeus son of Timaeus, a blind beggar, was sitting by the roadside."

If we allow our imagination to help us in our search for Jesus, we can hear the blind beggar describe what happened to him in his own words:

"I, Bartimaeus, was a successful carpenter. I was much respected in my village for my skill and had acquired enough money to live comfortably and to put some aside for a later time. I was faithful in my religious practice, observing all the feast days and the other commandments of the Law. Indeed, in the synagogue I was often asked to read from the scroll. On the Sabbath I would relax with my friends; I had many friends. My only regret was that I had never found a woman I wanted to marry, and I had no children. My friends, especially among other craftsmen, made up for my lack of a wife and family. Yet I considered myself to have been blessed by God. I looked forward to a life of continued satisfactions and a venerable old age.

"One day a wood chip entered my right eye, destroying it. A few weeks after the wound had healed, for some reason my sight began to fail in my left eye. In six months, I was totally blind. Fortunately, I could afford to live for another six months without working. During this time, I tried to obtain help from my few relatives. However, because of an ancient con-

3

flict between them and my father, now deceased, they offered no help. When it came to helping me with money, my friends proved to be less friendly than they had been. I discovered that casual companionship was not the same thing as true friendship. Though I did not have to worry about supporting a wife and children, I did have to worry about supporting myself.

"I complained to the Lord. 'Why have you let this happen to me? Haven't I always been faithful in observing the Sabbath and feast days? Haven't I given my tithes? Haven't I been generous with the poor? Now I will have to be a beggar at the side of the road.' Even remembering the story of Job was little consolation to me. I began to think that God had abandoned me.

"One day as I sat begging by the side of the road, I heard a commotion. 'What is that noise?' I called out, knowing that some nearby people would hear me. 'It is Jesus from Nazareth,' someone replied. I had heard rumors about a new teacher, going about healing people. I had heard that he was a descendant of David and that some believed him to be a Messiah. Rumor also said that the authorities were not pleased with him.

"For my part, it didn't matter what his politics might be. All that mattered was that he had a reputation as a healer. When the noise came nearer, I called out, 'Jesus, Son of David, have mercy on me!' The crowd at first told me to hold my tongue. They saw me as merely a nuisance, another beggar intruding with his demands. Then they told me to come over to him because Jesus had said, 'Call him here.' When I came to him, Jesus asked me, 'What do you want me to do for you?' In some strange way, his voice moved me inside so that I really believed he could and would help me. I immediately replied, 'My teacher, let me see again.' Jesus then said, 'Go; your faith has made you well.'

"Suddenly, I could see! My first vision after regaining my sight was the one who had healed me. He was looking at me intently. There was love and compassion in his eyes. Everyone else had rejected me. Yet this man, a complete stranger, showed concern. Indeed, his manner was exceedingly kind. I decided then and there that I wanted to know him much better and resolved to be his disciple.

"From that time, I followed him in his journey through the towns of

4

Israel. I saw him reach out to heal many others as he had healed me. I saw him bring many others to see spiritually as well as with their physical eyes. My new-found spiritual vision was his most important gift to me."

There are many among us, including myself, who at one time have said, "we see" when, in fact, we did not see. We went along day by day and year by year, complacent about our relationship with the Lord. Then some catastrophe reduced our lives to ruins. That happened to me before I awakened from my chemical dependency many years ago. I thought that I was faithful to my calling as a priest and that I had a good understanding of Jesus from my earlier seminary studies. Yet, as I was to see later, I had lost the ability to minister effectively as a priest, and I had become an alien among my brothers in the religious community to which I belong. I began to see correctly only when my chemical dependency brought me to a crisis and Jesus delivered me from it.

Others of us may have lost our jobs and our homes because of an economic downturn or "restructuring" of the companies for which we worked. We may have lost our spouses because of death, or through severe mental infirmity or infidelity, theirs or ours. Like Bartimaeus, we may have lost our physical integrity or health. Along the way, it is likely that we also lost our self-respect and the respect of our neighbors.

A personal encounter with Jesus is a powerful healing experience. We may encounter him in the privacy of prayer. Some people receive a mystical knowledge of the kindness and power of the Lord. This kind of experience is not the same as the visions and the hearing of words with our ears which some saints have reported. Those are spectacular events. A more ordinary, yet mystical knowledge of Jesus gained in quiet prayer is rather a deep sense of the presence, love and power of the Lord. It is a conviction that Jesus is deeply concerned about us and is able and willing to help us in our needs. We become certain that he is faithful and will do what we believe he can do.

We meet him too in the compassion of his disciples when they help us to regain our sight, as Jesus helped Bartimaeus. It may be that Jesus prefers to work through others so that they might have an opportunity to become more like him, and we might learn to see him in the help they give us. An example is the account of Saul receiving his sight at the hands of

Ananias:

> So Ananias went and entered the house. He laid his hands on Saul and said, "Brother Saul, the Lord Jesus, who appeared to you on your way here, has sent me so that you may regain your sight and be filled with the Holy Spirit." And immediately something like scales fell from his eyes, and his sight was restored (Acts 9:17-18a).

Whether in prayer or through the kindness of those Jesus sends to us, we come to know a Lord who is full of compassion for us when we are in great need of his mercy. It is precisely when we have no other hope that he extends his mercy to us, as a human friend as well as God. He has a human touch because he has a human heart. He can heal our wounds because he is God.

⚜ PRAYER ⚜

Lord Jesus, there was a time when I thought that I could see. I did indeed have the use of my bodily eyes, and I had a mind that could plan my daily life for goals that seemed to make sense. Like Bartimaeus, I was confident that I could handle anything that might come along. Life then presented me with surprises which disturbed my plans. I found that I no longer had control over my present, let alone my future.

It was then that you inspired me to see that I really could not see unless you enlightened me. You have now become the light of my life. Past, present and future have a new meaning because of what you have shown me. Most importantly, you have revealed who you are and who I am.

I am in need and with little power by myself. You have all power to heal my soul and give me a life that has lasting meaning, while I follow your lead a day at a time.

I believe in your power and in your love. It was your love which first enabled me to see who you really are—a God of great compassion with a human heart of great compassion. Like Bartimaeus, I want to know you better.

From the moment that you reached out to me to help me in my great need, I have been grateful that you are who you are and that you have called me to follow you.

CHAPTER 2: His Father's Son

In his origins, Jesus is Son of God and himself God. He is son of Mary and thoroughly human. Both are essential truths about Jesus.

When Jesus healed the blindness of Bartimaeus, we are able to see his concern for a suffering human being. Moreover, we can see the humanity of Jesus at work in our world at the dawn of his ministry, as a sign of what he does even now, bringing the mercy of God into our midst. He felt the suffering of Bartimaeus then, and he still understands in a human way our distress in the world in which we live.

Some have seen Jesus as simply a good man inspired by God. However, John the Evangelist tells us that Jesus is the perfect image of the mind and heart of his Father. The Letter to the Hebrews, in speaking of Jesus as a Person who is both divine and human, tells us:

> He is the reflection of God's glory and the exact imprint of God's very being, and he sustains all things by his powerful word (Heb. 1:3a).

None of us can see the Father directly in this world. We know by faith that he is infinite, eternal and loving. But without his reflection in Jesus we would have only a poor understanding of what that means.

Thus, the Word of God entered our world and took our human nature. Jesus has a human heart, that is, he deeply feels what we feel. He is moved by our suffering, and our hopes and joys as well. It was the human Jesus who healed Bartimaeus. The human Jesus reveals the Father to us as patient, forgiving and merciful. He shows us a Father who wants all of us, even the most miserable sinners and outcasts of this world, to be saved and to live in perfect happiness with him. He shows us a Father who is willing to give us his own Son to make this possible.

We can ask: "What is the relationship of the human Jesus to his Father?" The human Jesus revealed that he is in perfect harmony with his Father. On one occasion, Jesus revealed the power within his ministry and his authority as Messiah in these words:

"I do nothing on my own, but I speak these things as the Father instructed me. And the one who sent me is with me; he has not left me alone, for I always do what is pleasing to him" (Jn. 8:28b-29).

Obedience to his Father's will was not merely one feature of Jesus' life and ministry among us. It was the center of all he did. He was continually moved to fulfill what he saw to be his Father's will. It is appropriate to say that his ministry was to manifest his Father to us in the saving work of our redemption and in every word which came from his lips. It was the Father who sent Jesus into the world to reach out with saving love and compassion in the Father's name to people like Bartimaeus. It is the Father who continues to reach out to us through Jesus, dwelling at the right hand of the Father in paradise.

To fulfill his ministry, Jesus needed to understand the mind and heart of the One who sent him. Some have thought that he had this knowledge from infancy, because Jesus is the divine Son of God. Yet, as the Letter to the Hebrews tells us, Jesus is like us in all things but sin (2:14-18 and 4:15). He had to learn like any other human being. He learned to speak by listening to his parents. He learned the social graces by visiting with his neighbors. He learned the skills of a craftsman from his earthly father Joseph. And it was likely that he learned the teachings of the law and the prophets in the synagogue at Nazareth.

Therefore, we can ask how Jesus came to understand the mind and heart of his Father. Jesus' inquiry regarding his relationship to his Father began early in life. When he was twelve years old, he remained behind in the temple to the consternation of Mary and Joseph. When they found him, he asked, "Why were you searching for me? Did you not know that I must be in my Father's house?" (Lk. 2:49). Mary and Joseph had found him "sitting among the teachers, listening to them and asking them questions" (Lk. 2:46). His answer to Mary and Joseph and his behavior suggest that he was exploring his relationship with his Father and coming to a deeper understanding of his mission.

Thus, Jesus was doing what youth at that age has been doing for all time and in every village and city. Though Jesus is the Word and, therefore, divine, it is evident that he was allowed to learn even the most important facts about himself and his life work in a thoroughly human manner. He was discovering that the Messiah had a saving mission to lead a world that was spiritually impoverished back to the Father. When the day came for him to begin to preach to his own people, he would say,

"The time is fulfilled, and the kingdom of God has come near; repent, and believe in the good news" (Mk. 1:15).

The good news was the word that Jesus heard from his Father, a word of divine compassion and hope for all of humankind, for the Father loves people of every time, place and culture. Jesus learned that he had been sent to proclaim the Father's love first to his own people and then to all the world.

The Father's relationship with Jesus is also meaningful for us. At the Jordan, at the time of his baptism by John the Baptist, Jesus heard a voice which said,

"This is my Son, the Beloved, with whom I am well pleased" (Mt. 3:17).

He would hear this again much later on the Mount of the Transfiguration. The love of the Father for Jesus was profound and intimate. The Father loved the human Jesus who reflected the Father's love in a human way. We can see in the love of the Father for Jesus the supreme revelation of how God loves each of us.

On many nights, Jesus gave himself over to prayer to his Father. We can only guess about how he might have prayed. Still, we are not without clues. In accord with Jewish tradition, Jesus would have given thanks and praise to his Father, on his own behalf and ours. In his awareness that he and we were loved so much, he would have responded with wholehearted love. Because Jesus was giving himself entirely to his Father's loving plan for the world, the unfolding of his mission undoubtedly entered his prayerful dialogue with the One who had sent him. For example, before choosing his apostles, he devoted himself to a night of prayer.

Later, in the Garden of Gethsemane and on the cross, Jesus would cry out to his Father in pain. That prayer reflected the perfect obedience and love for both his Father and us which was the center of all that Jesus said and did. Even in sorrow and desolation, the love of Jesus endured for our sake. The bond of Jesus with his Father was an irrevocable covenant into which we have been taken up in accord with the Father's saving will.

At the Last Supper, Jesus spoke of his divine origin and the work of his Father through him when he said to Philip:

> "Have I been with you all this time, Philip, and you still do not know me? Whoever has seen me has seen the Father. How can you say, 'Show us the Father'? Do you not believe that I am in the Father and the Father is in me? The words that I say to you I do not speak on my own; but the Father who dwells in me does his works" (Jn. 14:9-10).

It is the Father, then, who heals the sick, preaches to the poor and offers salvation to the children of God, through the words and actions of Jesus. That was true 2000 years ago when Jesus displayed the Father's mercy in many works of saving love for his neighbors, and it is true today.

❧ PRAYER ❧

Father of Jesus, our Father, my Father, thank you for sending your Word into the world with a human nature like my own. From the beginning you have loved me, creating me in your own image and giving me grace so that your image may become a more true likeness of you. You loved me even when my way of life was far from lovable. You were patient with me while I slowly learned to call you "Father" and trust you to lead me to my goal, which is perfect happiness with you.

Your Son Jesus was always obedient to you, with an obedience of love. He entered the world as a mere infant dependent on the care of Mary and Joseph. In due time, he was obedient to them as messengers of your divine will. Moved by the Spirit who proceeds from you, he undertook his difficult mission to redeem the world and bring the message of your love for it to every place and time.

Though himself God, Jesus, as the human Messiah, offered praise to you, Father, for your gracious goodness to little ones. He received them because you receive them. He drew them to himself and then to you because he perfectly reflected your acceptance and compassionate love.

Jesus trusted in you even in the hour of darkness, when the forces of evil seemed to prevail. You had promised him that you would raise him up and, with him, all of us. Filled with confidence, he took up his cross and prepared for you a holy people.

Your Son taught us to call you Our Father. May your name indeed be hallowed. May your kingdom come!

CHAPTER 3: SON OF MARY

In the Annunciation we see the Word of God, the second Person of the Trinity, taking our human nature. There always remains a mystery in the Person of Jesus. In this life, we can never have a perfectly clear understanding of the answer to the question "Who is Jesus?" It would be a serious mistake to try to understand him as simply divine or simply human. The heart of Jesus went to great lengths to convince us that he is human as well as divine.

Thus, Jesus is not only the Son of the heavenly Father and himself God, but in his human nature he is the son of Mary. He did not merely dwell within her for nine months. Mary was truly his mother. She gave him his body, and she educated his human mind and heart.

When Gabriel announced the birth of Jesus, Mary shared her people's expectation that the Messiah would come and receive "the throne of his ancestor David" (Lk. 1:32). In David's time, the people had been relatively faithful to their covenant with God, they had been freed from their enemies, and they had enjoyed prosperity. Mary could see in Jesus the fulfillment of longstanding promises. However, his conception by the Holy Spirit mystified her. She had to take the *how* of Jesus' coming on faith.

Like her son, Mary was always responsive to the work of the Holy Spirit within her heart. When Jesus would say, much later, that he always did the Father's will, his words remind us of those of his mother when she said to Gabriel:

"Here am I, the servant of the Lord; let it be with me according to your word" (Lk. 1:38).

Mary's visit to Elizabeth reveals for the first time the power of Jesus to bring holiness into the world. The Holy Spirit entered Elizabeth, causing her to proclaim the mercies of God to her cousin Mary, and moved John the Baptist in her womb. The Holy Spirit also inspired Mary. All three prophesied in their own ways, John by quickening in the womb of Elizabeth. Jesus still sends the Holy Spirit into individual lives and into the world.

Nowhere is the humanity of Jesus more evident than in the crib in Bethlehem. Francis of Assisi was so moved by this scene that he instituted the practice of commemorating Jesus' birth with a creche at Christmas. Francis understood that, before God, we are all infants no matter what our age. The helplessness of Jesus is a symbol of our inability to achieve spiritual perfection merely by our own efforts. Jesus began his career as a helpless infant and completed his mission as a victim nailed to a cross, unable to move hand or foot. For one who had the power to transform the world, that is truly marvelous. Of course, it was the human Jesus who shared our helplessness while he dwelt among us, and the divine Jesus who had and has all power.

Francis also saw in the poverty of Bethlehem a foreshadowing of the poverty that would be a main mark of his own spirituality. Like Jesus' poverty, that of Francis extended to all features of his daily life. Jesus once said to a man who wanted to become his disciple:

> "Foxes have holes, and birds of the air have nests; but the Son of Man has nowhere to lay his head" (Lk. 9:58).

From the very beginning, Jesus has also given many signs of his preference for the poor of this world, from the shepherds who were privileged to hear the good news on that first Christmas, to the people of our day who live on the margins of society and receive his compassion through his disciples.

It is fortunate for us that Jesus is both human and divine. As the Letter to the Hebrews tells us:

> "For we do not have a high priest who is unable to sympathize with our weaknesses, but we have one who in every respect has been tested as we are, yet without sin" (Heb. 4:15).

Jesus is, therefore, able to suffer in our suffering and to rejoice in our joy, through all the ages. At the same time, because Jesus is God, he has divine power to purify us in this world and bring us to our fulfillment in paradise. Those of us especially who have been led into ruin by our own self will need a savior who is both divine and human. From his humanity, we can learn humility; in his divine power, we can find hope.

After his birth, we next meet Jesus at his presentation in the temple. He came into the temple in the arms of his mother, with Joseph his foster-father at her side, "and they offered a sacrifice according to what is stated in the law of the Lord..." (Lk. 2:24). Those of us who are gentiles often so rejoice in the universality of Jesus' saving mission that we overlook the fact that Jesus was firmly rooted in the traditions of his Jewish people. He would indeed confront some of them when they failed to see and love God. He did not, however, abolish what was sound in them. We cannot come to know the real Jesus unless we come to know him as thoroughly Jewish. His way, that of offering frequent thanks to God even in the midst of great adversity, reflects an ancient and modern Jewish way of prayer.

We meet him again in the temple at the age of twelve. On that occasion, as I have already noted, we find him exploring his mission. At this stage, he is an asker of questions, not a giver of answers, as some would have it.

There is another feature to this scene which is significant for understanding who Jesus is. His behavior caused Mary and Joseph great perplexity. First, he was not where they expected to find him. Second, his responses to them were inscrutable. In our own lives, when we seem to lose Jesus and then find him again, we reenact the experience of Mary and Joseph. Even after finding him, we may not understand what he is doing in our lives. Mary and Joseph needed great faith, and so do we.

After finding him in the temple, "His mother treasured all these things in her heart"(Lk. 2:51). By the time Jesus is ready to begin his ministry, Mary had come to a much better appreciation of her role in Jesus' mission. At Cana, Jesus deferred to his mother's intercession for their host. This scene, where Jesus gave a messianic sign though his "hour had not yet come" (Jn. 2:4), suggests the messianic fulfillment on Calvary, where Mary would again be a witness. Jesus favored his mother, not so much because she had given him physical birth, but because of her faith in him and total dedication to the purposes of his heavenly Father.

Mary was not only Jesus' mother; she was his first and most dedicated disciple. At one time, Jesus told a crowd,

> "Who is my mother, and who are my brothers?" And pointing to his disciples, he said, "Here are my mother and my brothers! For whoever does the will of my Father in heaven is my brother and sister and mother" (Mt. 12:48-50).

15

As Jesus' first disciple, Mary is now our teacher. She says to us what she said at Cana, "Do whatever he tells you" (Jn. 2:5).

Mary was near her son all the way to the end. Besides the sign given through the infant in Bethlehem and the sign given in Jesus' passion, there is perhaps no more striking example of the humanness of Jesus than his words to his mother and the disciple John standing at the foot of the cross:

> When Jesus saw his mother and the disciple whom he loved standing beside her, he said to his mother, "Woman, here is your son." Then he said to the disciple, "Here is your mother." And from that hour the disciple took her into his own home (Jn. 19:26-27).

In these words, Jesus showed that he had truly become one of us. He loved the mother who had borne him, and was concerned about her welfare after his death. He was concerned also about John and, through John, for all of us. Jesus was and is the son of Mary. By his gracious gift, we too are her children.

❧ PRAYER ❧

I believe that your mother is your ideal for me, Lord Jesus. She is also my teacher. She opened herself to receive you when you humbled yourself to come among us as a human being. She nurtured you as you would have me nurture the poor and all others whose face shows me your own. When perplexed she meditated upon what you were doing in her life, always maintaining faith in you. Mary was able to let go of you in your ministry, just as you want me to let go of everything else in the service of your mission.

Mary stood at the foot of your cross. That is also where you would have me stand, learning from you how to offer myself as a disciple, whatever sufferings discipleship may bring. She rejoiced in your resurrection. You would have me rest my faith on you as my risen Lord and rejoice that you have promised to raise me up on the last day.

Mary offered her prayers in the midst of the assembly waiting for Pentecost. You have called me into the great assembly of your Church to share in its prayer and mission. Finally, you have given Mary to me as my mother so that she can form me to become more like you.

Thank you for your mercy in giving Mary to all of us who follow you, and for giving us to her to cherish and love as a most pure reflection of you.

Chapter 4: On a Country Road

Now that we have looked at Jesus' origins, it is time to return to his journey through the Holy Land, bringing the good news of his Father's saving love. We will see him through the eyes of one of his early disciples:

"I am only twenty years old and have always been in good health. I didn't need the healing of my body, like some of the others who accompany us. I was an apprentice to a stone mason and had an assured income, though it was not much. Someday, I would be a master craftsman and could live comfortably for the rest of my days. Still, my soul was not at peace. There was something missing in my life. I felt a yearning for spiritual meaning. I did not find it in the religious practices of my childhood, which were merely a social custom for my parents. Our family worship was routine and lifeless.

"When I listened to Jesus on the day he came to our village, I recognized immediately that he was offering me an opportunity I might never see again. He stirred my soul and my heart by the way he showed concern for the beggars, the sick, and those like myself who had no spiritual bearings. I could see and hear that he was a man sent by God. He was the answer to my silent prayer for spiritual meaning.

"Today, we are walking along a dusty country road. It is about noon. We have just left my village, where the leaders, men of learning and authority, had rejected the message Jesus brought to them, urging the ordinary people to do the same. He wasn't a teacher with an established reputation. His origins were humble and his education that of a village carpenter. Most importantly he didn't tell them what they wanted to hear from a would-be Messiah. He offered no plan for solving the political or economic problems of Israel. Indeed, he called people to let go of their material concerns.

"Some of the inhabitants of the towns through which he passed ridiculed him as they had ridiculed John the Baptist. John, they had decided, was an insane and eccentric hermit; Jesus appeared to them to be 'a glutton and a drunkard, a friend of tax collectors and sinners' (Mt. 11:19). These people had been resistant to Jesus' proclamation of the good news in spite of the signs of his love which he had shown them. He has good reason to be downcast.

"Then Jesus looks around at us. He sees several fishermen, a former tax collector, a small householder named Nathaniel, a woman who had been a prostitute, a few beggars who had been blind and lame but now were whole again, and some folk who had simply been ready to hear him when he came to their villages. He also sees me. We exchange glances. He seems to know that I understand his frustration.

"A change comes over him. We lose eye contact as he seems to be carried away by an inner vision. He breaks out into a prayer of praise and thanksgiving:

> 'I thank you, Father, Lord of heaven and earth, because you have hidden these things from the wise and the intelligent and have revealed them to infants; yes, Father, for such was your gracious will. All things have been handed over to me by my Father, and no one knows the Son except the Father, and no one knows the Father except the Son and anyone to whom the Son chooses to reveal him' (Mt. 11:25-27).

"All of us are struck by the intimacy with his Father which shines through his words. Jesus has called himself the Son of God, and we have come to believe this. The present moment reinforces our belief. Jesus is also accurate in how he sees us. We are infants in spiritual matters. Until recently, most of us had not even been born in a spiritual way. Some of us had had very troubled lives. We groaned under the weight of our sins. Now we are free.

"While we are reflecting, Jesus seems to read our minds and continues:

> 'Come to me, all you that are weary and are carrying heavy burdens, and I will give you rest. Take my yoke upon you, and learn from me; for I am gentle and humble in heart, and you will find rest for your souls. For my yoke is easy, and my burden is light' (Mt. 11:28-30).

"I wonder what he means by his yoke and his burden. He isn't like the scribes and Pharisees who are always inventing new ways to control me and others like me. Then I begin to understand that what he asks of me is that I have the humility to follow his lead and live in peace with the others, whom he calls my brothers and sisters. Indeed, he calls all of us *his* brothers and sisters.

"Again, Jesus looks at me and I look at him. In his eyes, I see not only acceptance of me as a person but that he delights in my lowliness. Humility is obviously the door to his heart. He has chosen to give his love to me. The burden of his love is one I hope to carry forever, for it is a burden that gives me peace and joy.

"That is how I first discovered Jesus. I continued to learn about him as I followed him down many a country road. I will share one more story, about the day we came upon a band of ten lepers:

> As he entered a village, ten lepers approached him. Keeping their distance, they called out, saying, "Jesus, Master, have mercy on us!" When he saw them, he said to them, "Go and show yourselves to the priests." And as they went, they were made clean. Then one of them, when he saw that he was healed, turned back, praising God with a loud voice. He prostrated himself at Jesus' feet and thanked him. And he was a Samaritan. Then Jesus asked, "Were not ten made clean? But the other nine, where are they? Was none of them found to return and give praise to God except this foreigner?" Then he said to him, "Get up and go on your way; your faith has made you well" (Lk. 17:13-19).

Generally, all that Samaritans and Jews shared was a mutual contempt for one another. Each were aliens in the land of the other. Yet, here were nine Jews associating with a Samaritan. Sometimes leprosy was a greater cause of alienation from other people than ethnic difference. Their illness actually gave them a bond of fellowship.

Lepers were outcasts not only from cities and villages; they were outcasts from their own families. Only when they were healed could they return to those who had been their loved ones. The Samaritan leper was, therefore, doubly an alien when the band wandered into Jewish territory. Jesus, of course, knew this.

Jesus' heart was moved with compassion. He knew only too well the loneliness of being an alien, even from his own people, as recent events had shown. He had even been rejected by the people of his hometown Nazareth, when they misunderstood the spiritual meaning of his message. He told the lepers to show themselves to the priests, so that when they were certified as clean they could return to their homes.

Nine of them assumed that they deserved what Jesus had done when they found themselves cured. Jesus was a prophet of his own people, and they thought they had a claim on him. The Samaritan knew well that he had no claim, either as a Samaritan or a leper. He was indeed among the poorest of the poor. He was ready to receive Jesus and the good news of God's love and forgiveness. Jesus sent him home, though it is reasonable to believe that he returned to become a follower of the Lord, at least when Jesus was in Samaria.

Jesus does not need the gratitude of those whom he heals in body, mind or spirit. He knows, however, that his followers need to be grateful. Only the grateful have the humility to acquire a deep knowledge of the heart of Jesus and his Father's saving love.

❦ PRAYER ❦

Do you rejoice over me, Lord Jesus? Have I a heart, like your own, meek and humble? I know that you would not have me be meek in opposing the evils which afflict your poor, but that you would have me be meek in responding to injuries to myself. Your meekness always looked for a change of heart in those who injured you. You wanted to attract them to what was better, not force them. You attracted me even when I was unfaithful to you, seeking my will rather than yours.

Though you are divine, with a human heart which is pure, your humility is a call to me, who am not pure, to imitate your humility. Do you rejoice over me? Am I at least a disciple who recognizes his littleness and faults and who wants to become better with your help?

You offered your thanks to your Father. Through you I can see the love which sent you into the world to call me and all other human beings into the family of your Father, first purifying us by your sacrifice of love.

Through you, I thank the Father for your coming in meekness and humility of heart to redeem me and show me and all the world how to come to the Father. I thank you too for revealing yourself and your Father to me and to all the world in a great mission of love.

Change my heart, Lord, so that I may personally belong to you. Make me a herald of your good news wherever you send me. May your little band of disciples expand to include all the world.

Chapter 5: Zaccheus

Jesus' journeys often took him into towns which were centers of business and commerce, and the Roman Empire's local political leaders made sure that they collected a tax from the citizenry. The tax collectors were permitted to keep a portion of what they collected for their masters. Many tax collectors were greedy and dishonest. They were concerned with their personal gain rather than the welfare of the community and its citizens. The common people were no more fond of tax collectors at that time and place than they are now. Even tax collectors who were more honest suffered from the general reputation of their profession. Nevertheless, Jesus had also come to save tax collectors. Luke tells us:

> He entered Jericho and was passing through it. A man was there named Zacchaeus; he was a chief tax collector and was rich. He was trying to see who Jesus was, but on account of the crowd he could not, because he was short in stature. So he ran ahead and climbed a sycamore tree to see him, because he was going to pass that way. When Jesus came to the place, he looked up and said to him, "Zacchaeus, hurry and come down; for I must stay at your house today." So he hurried down and was happy to welcome him. All who saw it began to grumble and said, "He has gone to be the guest of one who is a sinner." Zacchaeus stood there and said to the Lord, "Look, half of my possessions, Lord, I will give to the poor; and if I have defrauded anyone of anything, I will pay back four times as much." Then Jesus said to him, "Today salvation has come to this house, because he too is a son of Abraham. For the Son of Man came to seek out and to save the lost" (Lk. 19:1-10).

For the religious leaders, Zacchaeus was a reprobate, whom they despised. Their criticism was based not only on the dishonesty of many tax collectors, but also on the fact that many of them did not fulfill the religious observances of the Law to the satisfaction of the scribes and

Pharisees. Ordinary people adopted their attitude.

He had heard rumors about Jesus. Others told him that Jesus was a miracle worker and prophet. The heart of Zacchaeus was restless, though he had a comfortable living. He dwelt in a fine house. He was able to eat well. He could provide for security in his old age. Yet, inside he felt empty. There had to be more to life than the ambitions and pursuits of his social class. There had to be more to life than money, comfort and security. Did he not have a soul that would sometimes awaken him in the night? He needed a deeper reason for living and hope for a more lasting future. He was troubled by unsatisfied spiritual yearnings.

Therefore, when he heard about Jesus' coming to Jericho, Zacchaeus wanted to see and hear this new teacher. He listened to the Lord from his perch in a sycamore tree, which he had climbed because he was short of stature. What he heard was the good news that Jesus had come into the world to lead it to repentance and eternal life. Moreover, he learned that Jesus had come to help people like himself, who were unpopular with everyone except other tax collectors.

Zacchaeus' good will toward the Lord suggests that, somehow, the Holy Spirit had been working within him. As a son of Abraham, educated in the Jewish tradition, he already saw God as perfectly just, good and merciful and could sense these qualities in Jesus' words. Thus, he could recognize Jesus' authority to teach the way to eternal life.

The work of the Spirit within Zacchaeus also made him willing to respond. Though faith does not come simply by willing it, it does need the absence of a barrier of unwillingness. To be heard and believed, Jesus needed the kind of willingness which he found in Zacchaeus. Frequently, the opposite was true. There were many frustrating days in Jesus' mission to the world. The popular reaction to his dialogue with Zacchaeus must have been frustrating to him. Moreover, not only his enemies, but even his apostles, sometimes misunderstood him. Luke tells of one occasion, when Jesus was traveling through Samaria and a town refused to receive him:

> When his disciples James and John saw it, they said, "Lord, do you want us to command fire to come down from heaven and consume them?" But he turned and rebuked them. Then they

went on to another village (Lk. 9:54-56).

At that point, it is clear that James and John did not appreciate that the mission of the Messiah was one of compassion and salvation rather than judgment. Jesus must have found them to be difficult students. Nevertheless, he persisted in educating them. Thus, they would learn to reach out as he was reaching out to all the people who needed God's mercy, even if for a time some of them resisted the good news.

We can learn how Jesus reached out to people from the scene in Jericho, when Jesus looked up at Zacchaeus and informed him that he would be his guest that day. Jesus was, of course, well aware beforehand of what the bystanders would say. He would know that some of them would not become his disciples precisely because of his acceptance of Zacchaeus. Yet in this story of Zacchaeus we can see how Jesus relates to each of us. He does not sacrifice his mission of reaching out to society's rejects because some people will be scandalized. Jesus was and is a missionary, and his work was to evangelize Zacchaeus and everyone else he encountered, whether or not they were held in high regard by their neighbors.

Early in his ministry, Jesus gave his disciples practice in their missionary calling by sending them forth two by two. Their task was not only to preach the good news to all the people they encountered, but to show the love and compassion at its center by healing the afflicted in the towns of Israel. He predicted that some would receive this message, and others would not. His disciples would relive the experience he had had when he offered salvation to Zacchaeus and anyone else who was willing to receive him on his terms.

Jesus' last act on earth as Messiah was to give his apostles and all of us a formal commission to proclaim the good news:

> And Jesus came and said to them, "All authority in heaven and on earth has been given to me. Go therefore and make disciples of all nations, baptizing them in the name of the Father and of the Son and of the Holy Spirit, and teaching them to obey everything that I have commanded you. And remember, I am with you always, to the end of the age" (Mt. 28:18-20).

Early Christians believed that Jesus had redeemed them personally from their sins by his passion, death and resurrection. Their own salvation was certainly central to the way they understood their relationship with Jesus. Yet, as the closing words of the Gospel of Matthew indicate, they also recognized the mission on which Jesus had sent all his disciples. This mission would find expression in distant places, and also among people closer to home who were in need of fundamental conversion, which had been true of Zacchaeus.

Immediately after offering Zacchaeus an opening to a new way of life, Jesus went to dine with him and his other guests. Scripture scholars have noted that Jesus often made use of dinners and feasts to meet the people to whom he wished to convey his message. In the story of Zacchaeus, it was at table that he met the other tax collectors in Jericho. He accepted invitations from prominent Pharisees. Jesus also enjoyed taking meals with his friends, whether in the house of Martha, Mary and Lazarus in Bethany or during his appearances to his disciples after his resurrection. He chose the setting of a meal to give us the Eucharist. If we look for the reason, it may be that there can hardly be an activity more human than that of eating. Jesus ate with *both* his friends and his enemies.

Thus, he instructs us that we too will find our missionary opportunities in the ordinary flow of daily life, including breaking bread with those around us. As believers, we will support one another in our faith. As witnesses, we will demonstrate the humanity of Jesus to those who need to find a savior who is truly human.

❦ PRAYER ❦

When you looked up into the sycamore tree, Lord Jesus, you saw not only Zacchaeus but also all of those who through the ages would consider themselves unworthy of you, perhaps because they had made themselves unworthy of you. Zacchaeus knew he was not righteous, as I too have known that I was unrighteous. Your acceptance of Zacchaeus was the sign of your acceptance of me. You have taken my unrighteous self and transformed it as you transformed Zacchaeus, calling me to leave my old ways and choose yours.

What great love when you look at me and ask me to invite you into my house! I have only to be willing to ask you to come and you will dine with me. Then I will be able to hear your words, and my heart will burn within me. What does it matter what the rest of the town thinks if you are with me? All praise to you, Lord Jesus, for noticing me and asking me to invite you to come to me.

Though you were the guest of Zacchaeus, in a spiritual sense he was your guest. I pray that I may acquire your gracious spirit and learn to be hospitable to those whom I encounter. When I break bread with them, I believe you will be in our midst bringing all of us closer to you and to our salvation.

CHAPTER 6: THE GOOD SHEPHERD

In revealing to us who he is, Jesus often compared himself to a shepherd. The role of a shepherd in ancient Israel was to walk ahead of the flock and lead it by attraction rather than drive it from the rear. In the evening, the shepherd would pool his sheep with those of other shepherds, and the shepherds would take turns guarding the sheep from the enemies of the night, particularly wolves. Then, in the morning, he would call them. They would recognize his voice. They would know that it was safe to respond to the voice they recognized. If one of them strayed during the day, a shepherd could have someone else watch his sheep, while he searched for the stray and carried it back to the flock.

Jesus gave us the most notable description of himself as the Good Shepherd in the Gospel of John:

> "Very truly, I tell you, anyone who does not enter the sheepfold by the gate but climbs in by another way is a thief and a bandit. The one who enters by the gate is the shepherd of the sheep. The gatekeeper opens the gate for him, and the sheep hear his voice. He calls his own sheep by name and leads them out. When he has brought out all his own, he goes ahead of them, and the sheep follow him because they know his voice. They will not follow a stranger, but they will run from him because they do not know the voice of strangers.... I came that they may have life, and have it abundantly. I am the good shepherd. The good shepherd lays down his life for the sheep" (Jn. 10:1-5, 10b-11).

In the figure of the Good Shepherd we can gain many insights into Jesus. One of the most prominent is that he draws us by his love instead of using force. He wants us to want to follow him. He wants us to exercise our liberty to choose his voice above every other. He seeks what is good for us and does not use us to serve some other purpose.

There were many false shepherds at the time Jesus said these words to his disciples. Some of them were political rebels who were willing to sacrifice the lives of their followers to achieve their political purpose. The Acts of the Apostles recounts how Rabbi Gamaliel told the Sanhedrin about Theudas, who led 400 men to their deaths. He also mentioned Judas the Galilean, another rebel who lost his life and his followers (Acts 5:34-37). In early Christianity, there were leaders who departed from the teachings of Jesus to found their own communities. The apostle John tells us in his second letter:

> Many deceivers have gone out into the world, those who do not confess that Jesus Christ has come in the flesh... (2 Jn. 7).

This pattern has continued down to the present day. In news reports in the late 20th century, we heard about cult leaders who led their followers to suicide. No doubt, they were seeking life. Yet anyone who was not a member of the cults saw the leadership and their goals quite differently.

Jesus said of himself that he had come that we may have life and have it abundantly. The Good Shepherd is life-oriented for his sheep, both in this life and in the next world. He wants to protect us from our spiritual enemies. He is truly concerned that we be able to live with dignity and a sufficiency of the goods of this world, as well as the grace which will lead us to the next. The Gospels offer examples of Jesus' feeding of the hungry and telling his disciples to do the same.

In regard to those who stray, Luke gives us a parable which shows how Jesus searches for the lost sheep:

> "Which one of you, having a hundred sheep and losing one of them, does not leave the ninety-nine in the wilderness and go after the one that is lost until he finds it? When he has found it, he lays it on his shoulders and rejoices. And when he comes home, he calls together his friends and neighbors, saying to them, 'Rejoice with me, for I have found my sheep that was lost.' Just so, I tell you, there will be more joy in heaven over one sinner who repents than over ninety-nine righteous persons who need no repentance" (Lk. 15:4-7).

Jesus' heart was moved to compassion by the spiritual aimlessness of many to whom he ministered. One such occasion is described by Mark:

> As he went ashore, he saw a great crowd; and he had compas-

sion for them, because they were like sheep without a shepherd; and he began to teach them many things (Mk. 6:34).

When hearing these texts of the Bible, it may seem that referring to human beings as sheep is demeaning. Sheep have been bred to be docile beasts whose only purpose is to provide us with wool and meat. We have the dignity of having been made in the image of God. In telling Adam to tend the Garden of Eden, God entrusted the care of the world to us. God has endowed us with intelligence and freedom, which make us capable of wisdom and love. We not only can but ought to make choices for ourselves. It is only in this way that we can grow spiritually and morally. How then are we sheep? What does Jesus see when he looks at us?

Intelligence and liberty to choose are not unmixed blessings. Intelligence can become mere cleverness, exploiting other human beings and the world in which we live. Liberty to choose can become license. Moreover, people can imitate one another in common folly, leading to collective ruin, as was the case in the cults who collectively committed suicide. In a less spectacular manner, whole cultures can destroy themselves spiritually by embracing values that cannot last. Jesus faced a materialistic society, in this regard much like our own. His society and ours seek treasures that will perish. Jesus called his hearers to a life that was spiritual and lasting by saying to them:

"For what will it profit them if they gain the whole world but forfeit their life?" (Mt. 16:26a).

The folly of many people whom Jesus encountered during his ministry grieved Jesus because he foresaw the negative consequences of their choices. On occasion, he wept over them. He longed to bring them to spiritual pastures where they could find the truth which would make them both wise and truly free.

The history of humankind shows that we do best when we have good leadership, even in the secular sphere. People generally do not believe that following a wise political and economic leader is demeaning. It is no more demeaning to follow the spiritual guidance of Jesus and those whom Jesus sends to complete his mission.

Though Jesus remains through the ages as our principal Good

Shepherd, he gave his apostles and all their successors a loving command that they be shepherds of his flock. He singled out Peter, but what he said applied to all. John paints the scene on the shore of the Sea of Galilee after his resurrection:

> When they had finished breakfast, Jesus said to Simon Peter, "Simon son of John, do you love me more than these?" He said to him, "Yes, Lord; you know that I love you." Jesus said to him, "Feed my lambs." A second time he said to him, "Simon son of John, do you love me?" He said to him, "Yes, Lord; you know that I love you." Jesus said to him, "Tend my sheep." He said to him a third time, "Simon son of John, do you love me?" Peter felt hurt because he said to him a third time, "Do you love me?" And he said to him, "Lord, you know everything; you know that I love you." Jesus said to him, "Feed my sheep" (Jn. 21:15-17).

In the gentle image of the Good Shepherd, Jesus tells us who he is and tells us as well how we, who are called to be shepherds in his name, can love him and continue his mission in the world. He offers a powerful attraction to the hearts of those who love him and are willing to serve. Many a missionary has sought or agreed to be sent to a distant place, enduring many hardships, urged by love and Jesus' words to Peter. Many a dedicated disciple, following the example of the Good Shepherd, has spent his or her life reaching out to little ones who have lost their way.

Understanding Jesus as the Good Shepherd may well be the most powerful motive for responding to his call to special service in the ministry of the Church. It is surely that for me. When I can lose myself in compassion for—and outreach to—the people around me in my society, I come to life in a way that would never be possible without my working as a shepherd. I am, of course, a sheep as well as a shepherd. Humility demands that I always remember that we are all sheep with a great need for the loving care of the Good Shepherd.

❧ PRAYER ❧

I hear your voice calling me at an early morning hour, Lord Jesus. You are saying to me that you want me to give my attention at the beginning of the day. I need this quiet time with you to insure the coming day against the temptation and struggles which it may contain. Now, I am not to trouble myself about them. In the hour when I need your special help you will be with me if my heart is open and responsive to you.

This moment of prayer is the opening of my heart to you and, more importantly, the opening of your heart to me. You offer me your strong support and share your desires and expectations with me. You call me to search with you for those who are not in your flock, whether they be people in distant places who have not yet heard of you, or people close to home who have forgotten that you are their shepherd.

Whether or not I am a person with a special call, I will have opportunities this day to be a witness to believers and others who do not yet believe. Make me your voice to those who need to hear it, Lord. Keep me attentive to your voice as I follow you this day.

Chapter 7: The Bread of Life

The Gospels make clear that Jesus is our teacher and our savior. He could be both of these while remaining at a distance from us. There are many examples in history of great leaders who have delivered their people from tyranny and proclaimed just laws to lead them to prosperity. These leaders have often been remote from the multitude who followed them. People can and do have confidence in the king who remains in his castle or the president who seldom leaves the White House. Few, however, would actually meet them, and they in turn may come to know few of their subjects or fellow citizens.

Jesus chose to do otherwise. Aloofness was never his nature, for it was always his desire to dwell among us and within us in an intimate manner. We encounter Jesus both as a community and individually, and he accomplishes this in a most remarkable way. He lives within our hearts, and he gives himself to us as the living bread of life in the Eucharist.

Jesus prepared people for giving himself to them in the Eucharist when he fed the 5000, as recorded in the Gospel of John. The reaction of the crowd was to see him solely as a source of material bread: they believed he would see to it that they would never again be in want. Jesus spoke of their expectation when he said:

> "Very truly, I tell you, you are looking for me, not because you saw signs, but because you ate your fill of the loaves" (Jn. 6:26).

Jesus had to draw their attention to the spiritual meaning of his miracle. He began to teach them about the bread from heaven:

> So Jesus said to them, "Very truly, I tell you, unless you eat the flesh of the Son of Man and drink his blood, you have no life in you. Those who eat my flesh and drink my blood have eternal life, and I will raise them up on the last day; for my flesh is true food and my blood is true drink. Those who eat my flesh and drink my blood abide in me, and I in them. Just as the living

Father sent me, and I live because of the Father, so whoever eats me will live because of me" (Jn. 6:53-57).

The setting indicates that Jesus is addressing the multitude as a community although, of course, each must eat his body and drink his blood individually. As they shared in the miracle of the multiplication of the loaves, so they will share the Eucharist.

Jesus intends the Eucharist to be bread that nourishes his community and each member of it. When we share the Eucharist, we come into a closer bonding with the Lord and are bound more closely with our brothers and sisters in the faith. Jesus' acceptance of us and love for us engender mutual acceptance and love among ourselves.

It is absolutely critical for a true understanding of Jesus' purpose in the Eucharist that we appreciate its communal dimension. It is all too easy for someone who has received consolation from the Lord when receiving the Eucharist to believe that its purpose is entirely an individual relationship with Jesus. There are other people present, to be sure, but they can seem to be only circumstances. An individual and intimate loving relationship with Jesus is certainly important for our spiritual lives. For Christians, love is at the very center of the spiritual life. Yet Jesus made clear in the Gospels that he had much more in mind for those who shared the Eucharist than an entirely private relationship with himself. He would have us become united with one another in a bond of mutual love built on the foundation of our shared faith in him.

Thus, the Eucharist is, first of all, a celebration within the community of Jesus' disciples. In the course of it, we participate by eating the body and drinking the blood of the Lord. In this way, the passion, death and resurrection of Jesus enter into the Eucharistic community and into our personal lives. The liturgy prepares us to follow the way of Jesus, who said:

> "...whoever does not take up the cross and follow me is not worthy of me. Those who find their life will lose it, and those who lose their life for my sake will find it" (Mt. 10:38-39).

To Martha, Jesus said:

> "I am the resurrection and the life. Those who believe in me, even though they die, will live, and everyone who lives and

believes in me will never die" (Jn. 11:25-26).

Each day we die to whatever draws us away from God. Each day our lives come into greater harmony with the risen Lord. In the end, God will crown a process which has been going on through all our days. When we share in the Eucharist, we say "yes" to Jesus, choosing for ourselves what he chose for himself. We make this choice as a community and individually.

In the Eucharistic celebration, the community and each of us come to a deeper knowledge of who Jesus is in himself and in ourselves by listening to his word in the Scriptures. Jesus is in the word we hear, in the thanks we offer to the Father in Jesus' name, in the loving bond of the community and in the sacrificial offering of his body and blood for our salvation. In all these ways, we encounter his divine and human love. It is as close as we can come in this life to union with God.

There are those who do not believe, because they have not yet encountered the Lord in the outreach of the Eucharistic community. That outreach needs to be one of love and sincere concern. Jesus would have us imitate his example in feeding the multitude with ordinary bread so that they might understand the divine love which offers them heavenly bread. Mother Teresa is reputed to have said that the love with which we feed the hungry is more important than the bread we offer them.

In addition to those who have never been members of the Eucharistic community, there are those who have drifted away from the Lord for many years. They may eventually return not only because they want a renewed and intimate personal union with Jesus in the Eucharist, but because they want a sharing in the life of the Eucharistic community. How the community presents itself is critical for drawing them back.

We can see in Jesus' giving himself on the Cross the clearest sign of the greatness of his love for us. The cost to Jesus was immense, and Jesus knew beforehand that he would suffer greatly. Yet, Matthew tells us:

> While they were eating, Jesus took a loaf of bread, and after blessing it he broke it, gave it to his disciples, and said, "Take, eat; this is my body." Then he took a cup, and after giving thanks he gave it to them, saying, "Drink from it, all of you; for this is my blood of the covenant, which is poured out for many

for the forgiveness of sins. I tell you, I will never again drink of this fruit of the vine until that day when I drink it new with you in my Father's kingdom" (Mt. 26:26-29).

Jesus pitied us in our spiritual distress and hopelessness and gave up his body and blood in his passion and death so that we might be saved and drink the cup with him in paradise.

When we were enemies of God and one another, Jesus reconciled us by his body and blood. At the Last Supper, he prayed that we might be a Eucharistic community bonded by our mutual love:

> "The glory that you have given me I have given them, so that they may be one, as we are one, I in them and you in me, that they may become completely one, so that the world may know that you have sent me and have loved them even as you have loved me" (Jn. 17:22-23).

In gospel times, Jesus sent forth his disciples with this prayer. Jesus offered the prayer for their sake and so that their mission would be fruitful. They would show their unity not by agreeing on every item which came up in the early Church, but by the respect which they showed toward one another and, even more by the spirit of charity which prevailed among them. People would be able to see the love of the Eucharistic Lord in the bonds of love of the Eucharistic community. They would be inspired to want to belong to a Church which revered mutual respect, love and concern.

Throughout the ages, Jesus continues to send us forth to proclaim in every place what he has revealed about himself in giving us all of himself. He said, "I am the bread of life. Whoever comes to me will never be hungry, and whoever believes in me will never be thirsty" (Jn. 6:35). Here is perfect love. We are sent to share this insight into Jesus and his Father's love with the whole world.

✣ PRAYER ✣

When you give yourself to us in the Eucharist, Lord Jesus, you are calling us to give ourselves to one another and to the saving mission which your Father first gave to you. You would have us open ourselves to your passion, death and resurrection so that they might be active in our daily lives, conforming us more closely to you.

Like many who first heard you promise the Eucharist, we are open to your word and willing to follow you. This too is a work of your grace. When you ask, "Do you also wish to go away?" we can answer with Peter, "Lord, to whom can we go? We have come to believe and know that you are the Holy One of God" (Jn. 6:67-69).

Thank you for this marvelous gift which endures through the ages as a powerful attraction to the hunger of the human heart for a love that is faithful and divine. May those who have left your altar and your table heed this hunger within them and return to you to be fed with the bread from heaven and to rediscover their bond with their brothers and sisters in the faith.

CHAPTER 8: THE SUFFERING SERVANT

The Christian tradition has long applied the Servant songs of Isaiah to Jesus. The First Song proclaims:

> He will bring forth justice to the nations. He will not cry or lift up his voice, or make it heard in the street; a bruised reed he will not break, and a dimly burning wick he will not quench (Is. 42:1b-3).

This image of the Servant shows his compassion and is obviously a fitting description of Jesus, just as the Gospel writer Matthew believed (12:21). How many times Jesus was gentle with those who were bruised by their own failings! Early in his career, he was gentle with the woman taken in adultery (Jn 8:1-11). He not only did not condemn her; he treated her with respect.

Before his passion, Jesus manifested his compassionate understanding of human weakness when he foretold Peter's lapse:

> "Simon, Simon, listen! Satan has demanded to sift all of you like wheat, but I have prayed for you that your own faith may not fail; and you, when once you have turned back, strengthen your brothers" (Lk. 22:31-32).

A short time later, Peter denied knowing Jesus, not only once but three times. Luke tells us how Jesus responded:

> The Lord turned and looked at Peter. Then Peter remembered the word of the Lord, how he had said to him, "Before the cock crows today, you will deny me three times." And he went out and wept bitterly (Lk. 22:61-62).

We can only guess what was in that look. My guess is that it was a gentle reproach: "I told you so!" Peter was a bruised reed, because what had happened showed him a clear and most uncomplimentary image of his real self. After his initial grief, he remembered the other part of Jesus' prediction. Peter realized that Jesus had accepted him and given him responsibility for strengthening the others, even before his sin. That

41

commission showed not only love but a long-range trust of one who would, for a moment, prove untrustworthy. Later, on the shore of the Sea of Galilee, when Jesus asked Peter whether Peter loved him, Peter's conversion was confirmed. Jesus had gently led him to give himself completely and loyally to his mission (Jn. 21:15-17).

Another image of the Servant presents him as a bearer of light to all people, and as a liberator:

> I have given you as a covenant to the people, a light to the nations... (Is. 42:6).

This prophecy foreshadows the universal outreach of Jesus, the mission which is at the center of his coming among us. The text continues:

> ...to open eyes that are blind, to bring out the prisoners from the dungeon, from the prison those who sit in darkness (Is. 42:7).

Jesus cited this passage in the synagogue of Nazareth, proclaiming himself as the liberator whom Isaiah had foretold. Unfortunately, the people of the town, like many Israelites who wanted political liberation, did not understand him in the spiritual sense he intended. Even at that early time Jesus began to suffer persecution.

In the Fourth Song, Isaiah paints a picture of the Suffering Servant, and indeed the whole suffering people:

> ...he had no form or majesty that we should look at him, nothing in his appearance that we should desire him. He was despised and rejected by others; a man of suffering and acquainted with infirmity; and as one from whom others hide their faces he was despised, and we held him of no account. Surely he has borne our infirmities and carried our diseases.... but he was wounded for our transgressions, crushed for our iniquities. . . (Is. 53:2b-5a).

If we are to understand Jesus, we need to meet him in his passion and death. Indeed, we need the passion and death of the Lord to appreciate the glory of his resurrection. His glory actually began in the suffering which preceded it. As Jesus said at the Last Supper immediately after the departure of Judas:

> "Now the Son of Man has been glorified, and God has been glorified in him. If God has been glorified in him, God will also glo-

rify him in himself and will glorify him at once" (Jn. 13:31-32). Only a few hours remained before Jesus would begin to suffer. In Jesus' passion, we can see our own suffering and the suffering of the world, for Jesus identifies with all of us. In a way which the world does not understand, the glory of God would be in the suffering. This is the secret meaning of Christian suffering throughout the ages, a meaning which has been a consolation to many Christians in every age.

We can also see sin for what it is and, above all, we can see the immensity of Jesus' love for his Father and for us. He showed his love for his Father by willingly undertaking to enter completely into our human condition, bearing our sins and our wounds, and thus fulfilling his Father's saving will. He showed his love for us by giving us himself entirely—his very life and, at the end, his open heart.

The passion of Jesus has always been a scandal to those who do not understand that the ways of God are not our ways. Jesus and Jesus' career as Messiah are mysteries because God is a mystery. Nevertheless, a loving heart can begin to glimpse the beauty of God's way of saving the world.

In his passion and death, Jesus is not only the victim described by Isaiah. He is high priest, at one and the same time victim and offerer of the sacrifice of the new covenant. Therefore, to know who Jesus is, we have to come to know him as a priest.

As priest, he is a bridge between the divine and the human. He brings the divine into our human world and lifts it up into the divine. Jesus' purpose is always an exalted purpose. In trying to understand any particular response to our prayers, it is necessary to remember that Jesus is always concerned with our ultimate destiny above all else. He wants us to share the very life of God, which he has opened to us by his sacrifice of himself.

Jesus enters into our ministries to one another, enabling us to have a part in his priestly ministry to us all. He has made us a priestly people, assimilating us to his work as the great high priest. To the extent that we know who Jesus is, we will come to know who we are, individually and as a community of faith. The high priesthood of Jesus, reflected in us, is part of our persona.

Conversely, by contemplating what Jesus is doing in us and in our community of faith we come to a better understanding of the one whom we reflect. By his grace, we see him mirrored in ourselves, not only at the time of formal worship but in all of our daily lives. Our suffering is his suffering; our praise is his praise; our thanksgiving is his thanksgiving; our mercy is his mercy. Through us he perpetually offers a sacrifice of praise and thanksgiving to his Father. Through us Jesus also reaches out to all the world, bringing all humankind into an assembly of praise for the Father who sent him as our high priest.

❖ P R A Y E R ❖

Lord Jesus, your people suffered great hardships and persecution from the beginning of their history, down to your stay among them, and beyond. The whole people has been a suffering servant of the one, true God. He is a pure spirit who will have nothing to do with pagan idols. Thus he had been hated and his people hated with him. The Letter to the Hebrews says of you:

He is the reflection of God's glory and the exact imprint of God's very being... (Heb. 1:3).

How could you not be hated? How could you not be a suffering servant?

Am I, as a disciple, to expect anything different? If I am faithful to you and to the Father who sent you I must be willing to put on the mantle of the suffering servant. There will be many opportunities in a world that does not understand what you have revealed and I believe. Only when I am a suffering servant can I truly call myself your disciple.

Yet my flesh is weak, Lord. I know that you do not expect me to be braver than you were when you asked your Father to remove the chalice from you, if that was his will. You do expect me and all of your disciples to be faithful to the model you have shown us. Though you accomplished the work of salvation once and for all in your passion, death and resurrection, in a spiritual sense they continue now in your living body, the Church. You graciously call us to suffer in union with you. Thus, we become purified. In addition, we can join our love and sacrifice to your saving love and sacrifice for your Church.

Thank you for the privilege of being joined with you in your passion and for the certain pledge of being joined with you in the resurrection.

Chapter 9: The Gardener

The Lord whom we seek to know better is now a risen Lord. Though he once suffered, he can now suffer no more in his own human nature. Yet he can suffer in us, whom he has chosen to be members of his body in a spiritual manner. Thus, Jesus could ask Saul, who imprisoned both men and women who believed that Jesus was their promised Savior:

"Saul, Saul, why do you persecute me?" (Acts 9:4b).

When we suffer for our faith in Jesus Christ, he suffers with us.

In the other direction, we have been raised from the dead with him in a spiritual manner. Indeed, we reenact his passion, death and resurrection every day of our lives. Each day we suffer the trials of our earthly life, each day we die to our self-will and its fruits. Each day, Jesus leads us to a new level of spiritual growth and union with the Father, Son and Holy Spirit. In the Gospel of John, Jesus spoke of this union when he said:

"I will not leave you orphaned; I am coming to you. In a little while the world will no longer see me, but you will see me; because I live, you also will live. On that day, you will know that I am in my Father, and you in me, and I in you. They who have my commandments and keep them are those who love me; and those who love me will be loved by my Father, and I will love them and reveal myself to them" (Jn. 14:18-21).

Jesus commandments are to love God and love one another. Founded on our faith and hope in him, we are bonded with the risen Lord by love for him and our neighbor.

Jesus revealed himself to his disciples immediately after his resurrection. On the first day he appeared to Mary Magdalene, and later to the disciples on the road to Emmaus. Mary's behavior when she encountered Jesus outside the tomb sheds light on our own relationship with the Lord:

As she wept, she bent over to look into the tomb; and she saw two angels in white, sitting where the body of Jesus had been lying, one at the head and the other at the feet. They said to her, "Woman, why are you weeping?" She said to them, "They have taken away my Lord, and I do not know where they have laid him." When she had said this, she turned around and saw Jesus standing there, but she did not know that it was Jesus. Jesus said to her, "Woman, why are you weeping? Whom are you looking for?" Supposing him to be the gardener, she said to him, "Sir, if you have carried him away, tell me where you have laid him, and I will take him away." Jesus said to her, "Mary!" She turned to him and said to him in Hebrew, "Rabboni!" (which means Teacher). Jesus said to her, "Do not hold on to me, because I have not yet ascended to the Father" (Jn. 20:11b-17a).

Mary's search for Jesus calls to mind the search of the beloved in the Song of Songs. We too may search for the Lord and find only an empty tomb. Then, when we are almost ready to give up hope of finding him, we hear his voice in our hearts, calling us by name. In this Jesus reveals a mystical communion with those whom he loves and who love him. Our tendency, like that of Mary, will be to cling to him. Yet, Jesus would have us be content with holding him by faith even when we cannot hold him.

Thus, when we also come to the empty tomb in our spiritual lives, as Mary Magdalene did, Jesus asks us to believe in his resurrection and our own. This is a great trial for those of us who, like Mary Magdalene, have been accustomed to consolation in our personal relationship with Jesus. This may occur during prayer. In the darkness and dryness into which we are sometimes plunged, we may feel that Jesus has been taken away from us. In fact, we are merely discovering him in a more perfect way.

We can ask why Mary Magdalene did not at first recognize Jesus. One reason was undoubtedly that she was not ready to encounter a risen Lord. Another reason suggested by the Gospels is that he was changed in appearance. It is difficult to understand how Mary Magdalene could have mistaken him for a gardener when she was looking directly at him if Jesus had not been changed in a significant way.

At one time, I entertained the notion that the risen Jesus had become, in some way, universal—that he is male-female, Jewish-Gentile, African-Asiatic-European-Other. That notion would fit in with the fact that Jesus identifies himself with all of us and that his mission is universal. It might also help explain Mary Magdalene's difficulty in recognizing the risen Jesus. Yet my idea is unlikely to withstand theological scrutiny. Jesus was a Jewish male and, we may reasonably believe, remained so after his resurrection, though his body has been somehow transformed.

I still treasure the nucleus of truth in my prayerful whimsy. In addition to his identification with women as well as men and with people of every race, all of us are equally made in the image of God and manifest human nature, the same human nature that Jesus took to himself. In a spiritual sense, we can find Jesus in all of us and all of us in Jesus.

By our prejudices we divide the image of God unfairly. Jesus would reconcile us with one another in a spirit of respect and mutual cooperation. That would not only make our personal relationships much better, but would rid the world of wars resulting from ethnic hatred. His Holy Spirit enables us to see beneath the surface qualities which distinguish us to find the bond of community and mutual acceptance and love.

Soon after Jesus had appeared to Mary Magdalene, he appeared to the disciples on the road to Emmaus. They had heard a rumor about the empty tomb, but did not know what to make of it. They had become discouraged by the crucifixion of Jesus. At the time of their meeting Jesus on the road, they had lost faith in him. The Gospel of Luke suggests that their reason for not recognizing him was rooted in their expectation of a different kind of Messiah:

> "...our chief priests and leaders handed him over to be condemned to death and crucified him. But we had hoped that he was the one to redeem Israel" (Lk. 24:20-21a).

From the beginning of his ministry to that very moment, there were people who insisted on projecting into Jesus their own desires. That had begun as early as his preaching in the synagogue at Nazareth, where the townspeople at first heard what they wanted to hear. We can believe that many of them were people of good will, but they were blinded by their preconceptions. That has been true for many people of good will throughout the succeeding ages. Many disciples have set out on the spiritual journey with great plans of their own devising. In trying to discover who Jesus really is, we need to accept him on his terms, with his goals and with his plan for leading us to our fulfillment in him.

At the time Jesus encountered the disciples on the road to Emmaus, they were still completely bound by their idea of the Messiah and his mission. When Jesus explained the prophecies about the suffering of the Messiah, their hearts were burning within them, as they later testified. However, it was only when they had welcomed Jesus as a guest and shared a meal with him that their eyes were opened.

They discovered him, not by way of a spectacular sign, but rather in a moment of human intimacy. Jesus reveals himself through what is human. This is the basis for seeking him in one another—the main theme of the second part of this book.

The trial of the two disciples is a feature in the lives of all who believe they are in the care of God and then experience suffering and grief. Some may have believed that Jesus would exempt them from suffering and grief. Like the two disciples, their faith is shaken when they behold the cross of Jesus up close—when it becomes their cross.

Their doubt can be resolved only when they embrace the mystery that God is in their suffering. Then their hearts will burn as did those of the disciples on the road. They will find Jesus in the human compassion of other disciples, especially those with whom they have a more intimate relationship. Even Jesus was consoled by the presence of his mother and the apostle John at the foot of the cross.

Jesus' purpose through it all is to raise us up. While we are on the way in this world, Jesus asks us to enter ever more deeply into his love, as preparation for our own resurrection into eternal life.

❧ PRAYER ❧

Lord Jesus, you see our world torn by racial and ethnic hatred. People reject one another because of differences which are equally expressions of our common human nature. The mere fact that someone else is different from me, or that someone's culture is different from mine, can tempt me to reject that person, even though he or she is as much your brother or sis-

ter as I am.

Until I can see you in people whose skin is of a different color than mine or who speak a different language than I do, I will be at least partially blind to your revelation of yourself. I believe you would have me broaden my vision so that I can come to know you as you really are.

You are a God of peace, and peace can only come when we are just to one another and respect one another. For a Christian that should be easy, but unfortunately it is not. Heal the wounds of our society, Lord. Bring us into a communion of hearts which share love for you and for one another.

The story of Jesus in the New Testament continues after his ascension. Of his direct personal actions, the most notable is his call of Saul to become the Apostle to the Gentiles, recorded in the Acts of the Apostles (Acts 9:1-20).

Jesus revealed himself to Saul by a voice which spoke out of a light from heaven. He said,

"Saul, Saul, why do you persecute me?"

Saul then asked the question which is the theme of this book:

"Who are you, Lord?"

The reply came,

"I am Jesus, whom you are persecuting. But get up and enter the city, and you will be told what you are to do."

For three days, Saul, blinded by the light which had shone on him at the moment of Jesus' visitation, sat in darkness, waiting. Meanwhile, Jesus called Ananias, instructing him to deliver Saul. Jesus told him,

"Go, for he is an instrument whom I have chosen to bring my name before Gentiles and kings and before the people of Israel; I myself will show him how much he must suffer for the sake of my name."

Jesus identifies himself with us. When we are persecuted or suffer in any way, it is as though the persecution and suffering are happening to him. Here again is a thoroughly human response on Jesus' part. He doesn't pity us from afar; he enters into our pain and supports us by his empathy and love.

Early Christians were subjected to pursuit and capture by men like Saul "breathing threats and murder against the disciples of the Lord" (Acts 9:1). Those who persecuted them thought that they were doing a service for God. Saul, no doubt, believed this. Jesus' opening question to Saul does not suggest that Saul was insincere. Indeed, Jesus appealed to his sincere desire to do the will of God. What Saul needed was education.

Jesus' instruction to Saul to go into the city and wait, and his allowing Saul to wait in darkness for the receiving of further instructions, shows his expectation of obedience from those he would deliver. Three days would give Saul plenty of time to review his life and beliefs and to mull over the implications of what had happened to him on the road to Damascus. Jesus communicated himself to Saul then and later as Jesus saw fit. It was Jesus' will that Saul begin his education with three days of waiting and in much perplexity and reflection. The proud Pharisee began to learn humility.

Finally, the words of Ananias regarding the suffering that Saul would bear for the sake of Jesus' name in his calling as a missionary to both Jews and Gentiles, show that Jesus expected him to walk a path similar to Jesus' own—passion, death and resurrection. Saul, now Paul, would soon begin to endure many trials.

To prove the authenticity of his ministry in contrast with false leaders who had intruded into the flock and were dividing the Christian community with their claims, Paul later wrote to the Corinthians:

> Are they ministers of Christ? I am talking like a madman—I am a better one: with far greater labors, far more imprisonments, with countless floggings, and often near death. Five times I have received from the Jews the forty lashes minus one. Three times I was beaten with rods. Once I received a stoning. Three times I was shipwrecked; for a night and a day I was adrift at sea; on frequent journeys, in danger from rivers, danger from bandits, danger from my own people, danger from Gentiles, danger in the city, danger in the wilderness, danger at sea, danger from false brothers and sisters; in toil and hardship, through many a sleepless night, hungry and thirsty, often without food, cold and naked. And, besides other things, I am under daily pressure because of my anxiety for all the churches (2 Cor. 11:23-28).

In the end, Paul was executed by the Romans because of his faith in and service to Jesus.

Following his conversion, Paul began immediately to learn the answer to his question "Who are you, Lord?" He went into the desert, where he heard from Jesus the message which would be Paul's own when he returned to Damascus. Even at that early time, Jesus may have told him that he desired the salvation of all peoples, including the Gentiles, by their faith in Jesus. Paul began by preaching to his own people, but soon began to reach out to others.

Throughout history, Jesus has prepared those whom he chooses to carry on his mission by letting them sit in darkness for a while and then find enlightenment with the help of another disciple. Often they then retire into solitude to explore the new understanding of Jesus and themselves that they have been given. Only then can they give themselves to actively proclaiming the good news to their disciples and to the world.

We can see in Paul's relationship with Jesus a reflection of the one who instructed him through visions and trials. Paul contemplated the passion of the Lord so frequently and deeply that the marks of Jesus' suffering were on his body. He wrote to the Galatians:

> From now on, let no one make trouble for me; for I carry the marks of Jesus branded on my body (Gal. 6:17).

He lived with a continual deep desire to be united with Jesus. Yet he also fully abandoned himself to the will of the Lord in regard to the ministry to which he had been called. Paul wrote to the Philippians:

> For to me, living is Christ and dying is gain. If I am to live in the flesh, that means fruitful labor for me; and I do not know which I prefer. I am hard-pressed between the two: my desire is to depart and be with Christ, for that is far better; but to remain in the flesh is more necessary for you (Phil. 1:21-24).

Paul was truly a friend of the Lord. His friend's interests were more important to him than his own. That could happen only if Paul experienced in a personal and intimate way the friendship which Jesus offered him.

Paul's solicitude for the churches also tells us about Jesus' solicitude for the churches. Jesus in the glory of the Father cannot any longer be anxious or troubled by the dissensions, factions, and petty rivalries of his disciples. Yet the mind and heart of Paul who was troubled reveal what Jesus thinks about the growing pains of his Church. He would have us live at peace among ourselves.

When we have become one in mind and heart, Jesus wants us to have his attitudes and desires and to become his witnesses in a world which very much needs to discover the Lord. There are many of us whose conversion and mission are hardly as glorious as that of the man we know as Paul. Jesus calls whom he wills, as he wills, and according to his plan which is always the salvation and raising up of his brothers and sisters—all of us.

With this story of Paul, who first met Jesus on the road to Damascus, we have completed the first part of our own journey by encountering Jesus in the Gospels and discovering who he is. We have been present with him when Jesus touched the afflicted with a healing hand. We have watched him develop in the loving care of his mother Mary and father Joseph. We have been with him at table while he accepted the hospitality of sinners and, much later, of his disillusioned disciples. Along the way, he gave us the bread of life merited for us by him in great suffering.

With Mary Magdalene we have grieved and been perplexed before we found him again when he spoke to our hearts. As a Good Shepherd to us now, Jesus has guided us to a deeper understanding of his love for us and for all humankind. Like Paul, we long for him, and we long to be and do what Jesus would have us be and do.

Nevertheless, even after we have contemplated Jesus in the Gospels and in his relationship with Paul, we need to remember that Jesus remains a mystery, for he is, after all, God as well as human. God's ways are often not our ways. God has a deeper vision of what is true, good and beautiful. Different people will see Jesus differently depending upon the life experiences they bring to their hearing of the Gospels. They are likely to emphasize different features of the Lord. Therefore, we need humility as well as faith in hearing the word of God. We will need humility too in our search for a true knowledge of Jesus, who lives and works with us in our present day world.

❧ PRAYER ❧

Lord Jesus, sometimes you illuminate us by a flash of insight. At that moment, we come to a deeper knowledge of you. Then you may allow us to sit in darkness until you reveal what you would have us do. Oftentimes in searching for our particular vocations as your disciples we pass through this sequence of light and dark. It is then especially that we need to trust you and wait patiently for your further enlightenment.

You called Paul to suffer many things for your name's sake. I believe that the only way to come to you and to remain in your company is to follow on the path you took and required Paul to follow—the way of the cross.

In my own life, the way has often been obscure. Generally, the confusion has been of my own doing. When you wanted to lead me to a better understanding of you, you have sometimes allowed me to wait in darkness until I acquired the humility to see you more clearly.

I pray that I may continue to find the truth about you and about myself in your light. I pray that I may have the courage to serve you, as Paul served you, sustained by your love for me and my love for you.

PART II: JESUS IN OUR DAILY LIVES

CHAPTER 11: A DIME'S WORTH OF GRACE

When we searched to discover who Jesus is from the testimony of the Gospels, we saw that he is not only divine but thoroughly human. Jesus himself had, and we believe has, a heart of flesh. He could love another human being with tender affection. The author of the fourth Gospel tells us that John was a beloved disciple of Jesus. The fourth Gospel also tells us that Jesus loved Mary, Martha and their brother Lazarus. He enjoyed their company when he visited their home in Bethany. Jesus wept for the widow of Nain. He had pity on the crowd at the Sea of Galilee and fed them in their hunger. He felt human weaknesses, including thirst at the well of Jacob, where he spoke with the Samaritan woman. Sorrow overwhelmed him in the Garden of Olives, and desolation engulfed him on the cross. He experienced every other human feeling, just like us, but he endured in a way that would encourage us in our own suffering.

We encounter the Jesus we meet in the Gospels both in our own daily lives and in the lives of those around us, particularly when we or they are in great need. Some of the most impressive demonstrations of Jesus' divine and human love occur in the lives of people who are addicted.

Many years ago, a woman told me her story of despair and deliverance. In listening to her, I could not be certain that what happened was due to Jesus' direct intervention. Nevertheless, the event that turned her life around was so unexpected and peculiar that I could not but suspect that the hand of the Lord was in it.

She had come from abroad to work as a domestic in New York City. She gradually became an alcoholic, and her alcoholism progressed to the point where she couldn't hold a job. She was on the streets, begging for handouts. There came a day when she was as disgusted with herself as many of the passersby who could see only a fallen woman in bedraggled clothing. Jesus, however, because he has a human heart, was concerned about her. He accepted her as she was, and wanted to help her become better.

She thought, "If only I had a dime, I could call A.A. and get some help to get me out of this way of living." She slumped in her old, worn jacket. Her right hand slipped through a hole in the pocket down to the bottom of the lining. There she could feel a small coin. When she brought it to light, she saw that it was a dime. She made the phone call, stopped drinking, and remained sober over all the years that followed.

Does Jesus pass out dimes to drunks on the street? I think it would be rash to assume that he never does. I have known many people like that woman, people who had been addicted and at the point of despair. I know of no other instance where the Lord gave them a dime. However, they have testified that their deliverance was the work of someone far greater than themselves. Occasionally, they have had spiritual experiences which instantly removed their obsession to abuse alcohol or other drugs, leaving behind a residue of character defects which they would have to work on for years to come. The Lord does want our cooperation.

These people frequently learn to spend a quiet time with Jesus each day so that he can continue the healing of their bodies and souls. For some, discovering Jesus on this level is so novel that they do not recognize their communion with Jesus as prayer.

A young woman who had been addicted but was so no longer once told me that she didn't know how to pray. She had been raised in a Christian household where daily formal prayers and Bible reading were customary. Later, when she drifted away from all religious practice, she forgot the prayers which she had been taught in her childhood.

She said to me, "In my quiet time with Jesus, I just talk to him and listen to what he has to say in my heart." What simplicity! Many monks and nuns would envy her prayerful relationship with Jesus.

I have known others too who have not been afflicted with addiction but whose lives had been spiritually empty until they were touched by the Lord. There was a doctor who had lost his childhood faith and did not regain it until his young daughter was cured of a serious illness by a faith healer. There was a priest who for many years had harbored a bitter resentment against another member of his order. On his deathbed he was visited by the man he resented. By the grace of God, the priest was able to let go of his resentment and forgive the other man. Thus, he not only died in peace; he gave Jesus' peace to his brother.

The stories of those whom Jesus has healed in our day provide an important insight to how we can discover and relate to Jesus when he reaches out to us in our need. We begin by realizing that we are miserable and cannot find any way out of our misery. We have tried many ways, and all of them have failed. We see only darkness, but Jesus sees an opportunity. Usually, it is only when we hurt enough to acquire some humility that Jesus will begin the healing of our souls.

Then, he will ask for faith that he loves us and is able and willing to help us. This is the point where we need to encounter him prayerfully in our hearts. There is no way to describe this encounter to someone who has not experienced it. Perhaps it can best simply be called "a sense of the goodness of the Lord." We say within ourselves, "I am miserable. He is kind. He wants to help me. He wants me to believe in him."

Jesus will help us on his own terms. He will certainly want us to let go of whatever separates us from him—our sins and other attachments which are destroying us. He will also want us to let go of our preconceived ideas about how we are to be healed. Then, his healing power will work in us and we will find a new way of life. We will also find a new way of looking at Jesus which can be quite different from our way of doing so in the past, even in a religious childhood. Our image of Jesus will grow up, as we become spiritually more mature and acquire a better understanding of him from our experience.

Our way of seeing him in the Bible will also change. For example, most Christians have heard the story of Bartimaeus recounted earlier. Many will see this story as merely one more example of Jesus' healing power. Those of us who have been blind, physically or spiritually, and have received our sight again, will see the story quite differently. It will become a personal event. It will further enhance our relationship with the Lord, just as it greatly affected Bartimaeus' relationship with the Lord.

When those who have been trapped by sin or some other harmful attachment read Paul's account of his own struggle with the evil within him in the Letter to the Romans, they will feel his anguish:

> For we know that the law is spiritual; but I am of the flesh, sold into slavery under sin. I do not understand my own actions. For I do not do what I want, but I do the very thing that I hate.... Wretched man that I am! Who will rescue me from this body of death? Thanks be to God through Jesus Christ our Lord! (Rom. 7:14-15, 24-25a).

Paul met Jesus on the road to Damascus, after Jesus had risen and ascended into heaven. He was a latecomer as we are, though a more exalted one. When Paul, with all his weaknesses, encountered Jesus, he also discovered Jesus on a very deep level as his loving savior.

❦ PRAYER ❦

When you took our human nature to yourself, Lord Jesus, you made it possible for us to become fully human. We had lost our innocence. Hearts that were made to love you and one another had, at times, become hearts of stone. You melted our hardness of heart by a gentle invitation to love you and to love one another because you have loved us. Now, day by day, you lead us by the bonds of love.

When I contemplate your revelation of who you really are in the opening of your heart to the world as you hung upon the cross, I am filled with dismay at my own occasional distrust of your concern for me. Forgive me this fault. Make me trustworthy in your service so that others may see your trustworthiness in my untiring compassion for them.

You have taken to yourself a truly human heart, filled with a human love which reveals your divine love. I praise your Father and you, in the Holy Spirit, because you have renewed our humanity in your own and made it possible for us to share in your divinity.

Chapter 12: Phyllis and George

Jesus reveals himself in every human being we meet along our path in life. On some paths, however, it is especially easy to see the qualities which the Gospels tell us are marks of his presence. One of these paths is personal experience of the Lord at the moment of conversion. That is why Part II of this book began on that theme.

Another way to discover Jesus is to see him in the mirror of Christian marriage. There Jesus is present not only in the individual spouses but in their relationship as well. He forms the bond which makes them one in heart, if not always in mind. For this reason, our search for Jesus in the daily lives of people loved by God looks next into his reflection in married love.

On the Feast of Epiphany, in a prayer that priests offer in the morning, there is a passage which reads:

> Today, the Bridegroom claims his bride, the Church, since Christ has washed her sins away in Jordan's waters; the Magi hasten with their gifts to the royal wedding; and the wedding guests rejoice, for Christ has changed water into wine, alleluia.

In this figure, the Church sees herself as the bride of Jesus, rejoicing in her spouse. She sees herself as having been purified by him to prepare her for nuptial union with him. She proclaims him her king, deserving of receiving wedding gifts worthy of a king. She recalls the wine of his blood which he shed for his bride on the cross. In his letter to the Ephesians, Paul took up this theme when he wrote:

> Husbands, love your wives, just as Christ loved the church and gave himself up for her, in order to make her holy by cleansing her with the washing of water by the word, so as to present the church to himself in splendor, without a spot or wrinkle or anything of the kind—yes, so that she may be holy and without blemish. In the same way, husbands should love their wives as they do their own bodies. He who loves his wife loves himself. For no one

ever hates his own body, but he nourishes it and tenderly cares for it, just as Christ does for the church, because we are members of his body. For this reason a man will leave his father and mother and be joined to his wife, and the two will become one flesh. This is a great mystery, and I am applying it to Christ and the church (Eph. 5:25-32).

Christian marriage, therefore, finds its model in Jesus' relationship with the community of his disciples and with each of us individually. Jesus' love embraces the assembly and each of its members. Conversely, Christian marriage is the mirror, already noted, which enables us to know Jesus better, for his love is at the center of marriage.

Phyllis and George Morris stand out as an example of a couple whose married life reflected the love of the Lord. Phyllis is now a widow after many years of marriage. I have known them during their retirement years, and before, during and after George's terminal illness. Because they loved one another wholeheartedly, they placed one another's welfare at the center of their lives, losing themselves in each other. From the beginning, they intended their marriage to be forever. Long after George died, Phyllis still styled herself as Mrs. George Morris. For her, George is not really dead, merely away on a long journey where she will follow him someday. They were always faithful to each other. It would never have crossed the mind of either of them to betray the trust of the other. They were bound so closely that their hearts had become one.

Their affection was radiant. It showed itself in the gentle, humorous and mutually supportive way in which they spoke to one another and presented themselves as a couple to others. When they were present together in a group, others could feel the joy in their marriage.

They raised their children in the faith which had been handed down to them, fully convinced that they were their children's first teachers in the way of the Lord. They were active in their church community, especially in reaching out to the poor of the area in which they lived. They offered themselves to the service of shut-ins and others who were in need of companionship as well as providing other help. Because they were retired, it was readily possible for them to carry on this ministry of compassion, and they made full use of the opportunity.

The loving relationship of Phyllis and George with Jesus enhanced their ability to give themselves entirely to one another, to their family and even to strangers in need. Their marital love was covenanted and blessed because of Jesus' presence to them as a couple. Thus, their union was one which already shared in the ultimate happiness which Jesus has promised to those who are faithful to him and to one another.

Their marriage had times of anxiety and disappointment. No marriage can be idyllic in the real world. Nevertheless, their love prevailed over all difficulties.

I have known married couples who were confronted with the chronic illness of one of the partners, or chronic illness on the part of a child. There have been parents who discovered that their offspring were homosexual, and who had to learn to love and accept them as their sons and daughters in a society which is frequently hostile to homosexuals. Other parents have had to face the addictions of their children. Their support during a time of recovery is critical to the future welfare of children who have become trapped by chemical dependency.

Perhaps the greatest trial of all for parents is their children's and grandchildren's drifting away from religion as they pass through their teen years. In the modern world, this is becoming an increasingly common burden. The immediate parents may blame themselves, in spite of the fact that they have lived an example which ought to have had another outcome. Fortunately, the religious drifting of their offspring is sometimes a transient event. Yet, this challenge and others can gravely test the quality of the love between the father and mother, who may not always see eye to eye about how to respond to this and other problems among their children. In a good marriage, the spouses learn to give priority to the marriage itself. It is the foundation of everything else in their family.

We can see a reflection of Jesus even in the disappointments and sorrows of spouses and parents. The love and patience with which they face them show us Jesus' love and patience with us all, even with the apostle who betrayed him. He loved Judas to the end, and called him "friend." He was patient with Peter, though he was well aware of Peter's weakness, which led to denial of Jesus for a time.

We may not be consistently faithful to Jesus, but his love for each of us is like that of a devoted spouse, though it is entirely spiritual. When we give him an opportunity, Jesus comes so close to us that we begin to understand what he thinks, feels and is doing in us and our world. We become his intimate friends. He reveals himself to us not in a spectacular way, but much more subtly. His peace abides in our hearts. We know that he is with us in every circumstance of our lives.

Whether we be married or unmarried, we can thank Jesus for the splendor of a holy and happy Christian marriage. In it, he reveals himself to us as a lover who gives himself completely and is always faithful. As a priest, I have often been restored in spirit by contemplating the joy and love of the married couples, like Phyllis and George, to whom I minister. I have been able to bask in their warmth, so to speak, of the glow of Jesus in their lives. They show me, too, how to be a faithful servant of the Lord and how to love those who are in my spiritual care in Jesus' name.

❦ PRAYER ❦

Lord Jesus, your love for us is so tender and intimate that it has been called spousal love. You anticipated your nuptials symbolically at Cana, where you changed water into wine at the request of your mother, though you said, "My hour has not yet come" (Jn. 2:4b). On the cross, the hour of your glory had come and you celebrated your nuptial union with us, again with your mother close by.

Love inevitably entails sacrifice. There was never a greater sacrifice than yours, nor a greater love. You have graced marriage as an image of your spousal love. We pray that couples may find in you one who understands their love for one another and blesses it. May they be witnesses before the world to what love of man and woman can be when it is blessed by you. Sustain married couples in their sacrifices and bring them to the great nuptial feast in paradise.

Bless their families also, for these are the fruit of their love. When their children wander, gently draw them back to your heart, attracting them by the bonds of love. Console those who have commended themselves and their families to you. Strengthen their love for one another and empower them to give witness to you by the holiness and the faithfulness of their mutual love.

C~HAPTER~ 13: K~ENNY~

Kenny, as he was fondly called by those who had come to know him well, was an urban hermit. When I first met him, he was about thirty years old, ten years older than me. Earlier in life he had been smitten with a desire to imitate Jesus' poverty in the style of St. Francis. He had tried to live as a Capuchin but had not been able to adapt to community life. That is how he became a hermit.

He had been raised on a farm, and his ideal was a life of extreme Christian simplicity, preferably one lived on a few acres of land. He would show me articles in a Catholic journal which promoted the notion of Christians going to small farms and finding their souls again. I believe he really wanted to do this, but he became an urban hermit instead because he had no money to buy even a small farm and he needed to support himself. He took odd jobs and lived in a tiny room in the basement of a tenement. He slept on a bare board and abstained from meat. Sometimes, his day-work employers would cheat him out of his wages. For Kenny this way of living made him more like his master, who had nowhere to lay his head.

Kenny took to heart the words of Jesus to his apostles:

> "Truly I tell you, at the renewal of all things, when the Son of Man is seated on the throne of his glory, you who have followed me will also sit on twelve thrones, judging the twelve tribes of Israel. And everyone who has left houses or brothers or sisters or father or mother or children or fields, for my name's sake, will receive a hundredfold, and will inherit eternal life" (Mt. 19:28-29).

When Kenny was not working, he could be found in a downtown church which was open most of the time. It was a church with a lower class congregation, many of whom were nearly as poor as Kenny—widows, pensioners and transients. He fitted in well with the people and the spirit of that church. Those who passed him in the aisles as he made the stations of the cross were impressed by his angelic smile. His piety was not only cheerful, but he had a sense of humor and could appreciate the odd impression he made on people. He wore a beard at a time when very few men wore beards. His choice was a statement about the softness and luxury of modern society.

When I left town to pursue my own vocation as a priest and religious, I lost track of Kenny. Many years passed. When I was in my fifties, I received a letter from him. He had found a bishop in the southwestern U.S. who had ordained him and appointed him as chaplain in a convent of contemplative nuns. There were few nuns and he had few duties. Kenny characterized himself as Father Dolittle, a play on the name of a well-known missionary doctor of the time. His sense of humor was still alive and well.

Kenny perceived Jesus as a simple, poor man living in joyous poverty among his people and, at times, in sorrow because of their lack of serious spirituality. Like St. Francis, he contemplated Jesus in his passion, walking with him daily along the way of the cross. Yet he saw that beneath the sorrow of Jesus was a deep peace. It was from that peace in possessing nothing but God that Jesus' joy would come forth at times, as when he offered praise and thanksgiving to his Father for giving him disciples like Kenny. It is easy to picture Jesus looking at him lovingly as he follows the master down a dusty road alongside the other trusting souls, willing to give up everything to become disciples of the Lord.

The vision of Jesus which impelled Kenny has had a powerful influence on Christianity during the past 1000 years. In the late Middle Ages, many groups of disciples abandoned the worldliness of cities and towns and went into the countryside to found communities where they lived with Christian simplicity close to nature. They rejected the established Church and its artificiality. For this reason and because their understanding of the gospel and its Lord was so very different from the prevailing view, they often suffered persecution. It was a time, it should be remembered, when many of the higher clergy lived in luxury and the material values of society often prevailed over those that were spiritual.

Nevertheless, even from the beginning, these communities had an attraction for those who remained in the established Church. In the mainstream religious world, monks, nuns and friars modeled their lives on the same understanding of the Lord. Francis of Assisi is perhaps the most famous example of a person who was in many ways like the rebels who left the comfortable Church for the wilderness. Indeed, he wanted to attract them back by showing them that they could live in harmony with gospel values within the Church. Kenny always reminded me of Francis of Assisi and taught me to see Jesus as Francis did. I did not follow Kenny's path because I realized that it was but one man's view, though a valid one.

Jesus often lived in temporary shelters. He received alms to support himself and his entourage of disciples. He spent his days on village streets and country roads, proclaiming the good news. Through the common purse held by Judas Iscariot, Jesus helped the poor. Indeed, that is what the other apostles thought Judas was doing when he went out to betray the Lord. His main apostles were fisherman rather than farmers. Yet their way of life was equally close to nature.

During my seminary years, I learned about Charles de Foucauld, and he too reminded me of Kenny. Charles was a contemplative whose first religious choice was a very poor Trappist monastery. Later, he went to the Holy Land and lived in a manner similar to that which Kenny had chosen at the time I first met him. Charles observed that the greatest contemplatives of all time were Jesus and Mary, and yet they lived among people and carried on the work of ordinary people. Eventually, Charles was ordained at an age older than usual and received permission to go to the Sahara to give a witness of the simple Christian life among Muslim tribesmen. The similarities were so striking that ever thereafter, when I thought of Charles, I would think of Kenny.

Over the years since I first met Kenny, I have come to believe that I was a romantic young man at the time and that he was a somewhat older romantic. He remained a romantic; I have since become much less so in my relationship with the Lord. For better or worse, years of ministry have made me more of a pragmatist. Pragmatists are satisfied with obtaining the best result possible in their ministry, whatever the ideal may be. That has also shaped my life style. I have to fit into the world in which I minister. It is unlikely that I will conform perfectly to Jesus' command in the Gospel of Luke:

> After this the Lord appointed seventy others and sent them on
> ahead of him in pairs to every time and place where he himself
> intended to go. He said to them, "The harvest is plentiful, but
> the laborers are few; therefore ask the Lord of the harvest to send
> out laborers into his harvest. Go on your way. See, I am sending
> you out like lambs into the midst of wolves. Carry no purse, no
> bag, no sandals; and greet no one on the road" (Lk. 10:1-4).

Still, I feel a tingle of pleasure as I write these recollections of Kenny.
He took the gospel command literally. He had once wanted to be a
Franciscan going forth in Jesus' name in poverty, while letting nothing
distract him from his service to the Lord. In his own way, he did fulfill it,
dedicated to its spirit all the days of his life.

I owe a great debt to Kenny for first showing me a new way to hear
the gospel message. I firmly believe that Father Dolittle is now with Jesus,
perhaps sharing a chuckle over this remembrance of him.

❧ PRAYER ❧

*Thank you, Lord Jesus, for Father Dolittle. You have made him a
mirror of your own simplicity and gentle humor. You have shown in him
your own poverty of spirit which chose actual poverty as the foundation
for your mission to the world.*

*How many souls, unknown in places of power and fame, are
known by you to be people after your own heart! In every age, they are
the disciples who give you a special delight. They are witnesses to how
you work in the world. Their mere presence, following you with total
trust, is a powerful sign to any who are willing to see it. Give me too a
heart that is trusting, simple and gentle. Give me a love for you and your
work in the world which sets me free from every selfish attachment. Let
there be no barrier between you and me and the hearts of others who
need to learn about you.*

*Free me not only from my sins but from the obsessions with the
things of this world which get in the way of my union with you and my
dedication to my calling and sending in your name.*

*Again, I thank you for Father Dolittle and all of the others whom I
have known who have brought joy and peace into my life by living lives
of joy and peace.*

Chapter 14: Bernice

Bernice had been an occasional volunteer in our monastery office. She had helped in the mailing out of appeals for donations to support our missions in Papua, New Guinea, and Colombia, South America. These are regions of the world where missionaries not only proclaim the gospel to the poor but also assist the people in their more earthly needs. Bernice was concerned about their welfare in this world and the next. Although she was Baptist rather than Catholic, she felt that her activity in our office was doing the Lord's work.

She was slight of build and had a gentle, peaceful disposition. One day she became ill with cancer, which was declared terminal. I went to her home, where she lived with her daughter, to offer her spiritual encouragement. I was warmly received by her and her daughter, and I soon discovered that it was she who encouraged me. Her smile was similar to that of Kenny's. Perhaps there is a smile that is characteristic of those who are close to the Lord. Whatever the reason, it glowed with her inner spiritual life.

Her faith in the love of Jesus was immense even though she knew that she would not survive the cancer. What she wanted from Jesus was not physical healing but the spiritual healing and support that only Jesus can provide. Her faith did not fail even at the very end of her illness. On the contrary, she spoke more fervently of her trust in him. It seemed to me that Jesus, on his part, dwelt close to her and that she was conscious of his presence, offering her the special support she needed.

When I sat with her in her parlor, together with her daughter, I was reminded of Tabitha in the Acts of the Apostles:

> Now in Joppa there was a disciple whose name was Tabitha, which in Greek is Dorcas. She was devoted to good works and acts of charity. At that time she became ill and died. When they had washed her, they laid her in a room upstairs. Since Lydda was near Joppa, the disciples, who heard that Peter was there,

sent two men to him with the request, "Please come to us without delay." So Peter got up and went with them; and when he arrived, they took him to the room upstairs. All the widows stood beside him, weeping and showing tunics and other clothing that Dorcas had made while she was with them. Peter put all of them outside, and then he knelt down and prayed. He turned to the body and said, "Tabitha, get up." Then she opened her eyes, and seeing Peter, she sat up. He gave her his hand and helped her up. Then calling the saints and widows, he showed her to be alive. (Acts 9:36-41).

I am not Peter, and I felt no inspiration to perform a miracle. More importantly, I realized that Bernice was not looking for a miracle from me or anyone else. It was not that she lacked faith in the power of the Lord. It was simply that she was completely abandoned in spirit to the will of the Lord, whatever that might be. Her spiritual instincts told her that Jesus was calling her, by way of his passion in her, to be united with him in paradise in the near future. I could see that she wanted to be with the Lord, not as an escape from this world but rather as an opportunity to come into the loving embrace of Jesus.

When Bernice died, I attended the wake. There was a throng from her church where she had been quite active, especially in the choir. The choir was present in their robes, singing the hymns which had been especially dear to Bernice. It occurred to me that their singing was like the women of Acts 9 displaying the garments which Dorcas had woven while she dwelt among them. The tone of the wake was more of joy than grief, though it was clear that those with whom she had worshiped and shared hospitality felt the earthly loss of her gentle and faith-filled presence. On the other hand, even the deceased Bernice seemed to be part of the choir that was singing in her memory. The wake was a celebration of life. Her life had been a success, and everyone present was aware of that fact.

While she was alive, I could see Jesus' love reflected in the care he took of her and in her response to him. There was intimacy in the dialogue of the hearts of Bernice and Jesus, evident in how she spoke of him. Yet her love was not merely a private devotion. She had reached out to others to share with them the great gift she had received.

In many ways, Bernice combined the best of Martha and Mary (Lk. 10:38-41). Like Mary sitting at the feet of Jesus, she listened intently to the word of the Lord spoken to her heart. By her service of love to others, she was a missionary of the one she loved and who loved her so much. That is what led her to be active in the choir of her church, inspiring her congregation to praise the Lord with an outburst of faith in their loving savior. That is what moved her to work alongside the missionaries of a Catholic congregation to bring the knowledge of Jesus to people in distant lands. First and last, she wanted Jesus to be known and loved by everyone, everywhere.

Her greatest service to others was her very presence and spirit. Others could see the joy she had through her faith in a loving Lord. Visiting with her, even in her final illness, lifted my spirit to share her joy in Jesus. I had not expected to find joy when I first came to visit her. I had expected to find a woman who was in great distress at the certain prospect of death from cancer. I found instead a serene soul who was a missionary to my own heart.

Bernice's vision of Jesus was in some ways similar to that of Kenny but in other ways quite different. Both saw the Lord as a man of peace, joy and love. Yet, where Kenny's view had emphasized the poverty and simplicity of Jesus, Bernice was moved by his very human spirit of friendship and hospitality, both given and received. Her faith and trust in Jesus as her savior and friend were especially evident in how she spoke of him and imitated him in his missionary outreach. She wanted to bring his salvation to others, so that they too could become the friends of Jesus.

I learned through Bernice a greater appreciation of the diverse ways in which Jesus guides those whom he loves. Because of her, I am more ready to allow the Lord to work as he wills. I believe that God wants each of us to search for the fullness of the truth revealed by Jesus and handed down to us in our day. I believe too that God wants us to embrace what we find. We don't make the truth; we can only discover it. Bernice's search confirmed her belief as a Baptist. My search strengthened my faith as a Catholic. We shared the same Lord and we could respect one another's sincerity and freedom of conscience.

At the Last Supper, Jesus spoke of the generous breadth of his

Father's embrace, when he said:

> "In my Father's house there are many dwelling places. If it were not so, would I have told you that I go to prepare a place for you? And if I go and prepare a place for you, I will come again and will take you to myself, so that where I am, there you may be also" (Jn. 14:2-3).

I firmly believe that Bernice is with the Lord. Though I am only a simple priest and cannot proclaim anyone to be a saint, and though we belonged to different churches, I have no hesitation in calling on Bernice to help me on my journey to the Lord. It may very well be that she is helping me write these lines, and so continuing her service to the Lord through her service to those who will read and meditate upon them.

From Bernice, I also came to a greater appreciation of the truth that paradise begins even now. She provided another answer to the question "Who is Jesus?" Jesus is the constant companion and lover of a simple soul who believed in him and loved him with all her heart. He is not merely the Jesus of history. He is the Jesus who is our savior and friend in the present moment, if we are willing to receive him as a guest.

❧ PRAYER ❧

Among your early disciples, Lord, you inspired a simple woman, Tabitha, to live in imitation of you "devoted to good works and acts of charity" (Acts 9:36). While the great ones of this world have created and destroyed empires, receiving the admiration and praises of the multitude, this woman was content to do your will in the simple works of love which have always so much pleased you.

You have called many men and women to follow in her footsteps, living quiet lives of piety and dedication to the good of others, in your name. They are admired and praised by the angels, who can see in them the flowering of your graces. Unlike Tabitha, their names will generally never be known to those who record the deeds of human beings in the chronicles of history.

Bernice received only a brief obituary in the local newspaper of a small city. Yet her life is written in my heart each time I think of her, and those occasions are frequent. I am sure that is true for many others in our small city.

Thank you, Lord Jesus, for your gift to us of such persons as Tabitha and Bernice. Only you know how many souls like theirs you have created and graced for the building up and delight of our spirits. They enlighten us and inspire us to live as they have lived, entirely devoted, because of their faith, to good works and acts of charity.

C<small>HAPTER</small> 15: R<small>OGER</small>

Behind the facade of a bungalow in a row of modest bungalows on a tree-lined street, a resident in a wheelchair slowly turns the pages of a book propped up before her by stroking them with a padded stick held between her teeth. Her arms and legs have long been useless. She is grateful that she can at least move her head. In the kitchen behind her, her mother prepares the evening meal. She will soon feed her thirty-five year old daughter who has been stricken with multiple sclerosis and is now in an advanced stage, in spite of her relative youth. On the other side of town, a nun sits in her small convent room reading a book in the same way as the young woman in the bungalow. A nun infirmarian will bring her dinner and feed her before putting her to bed for the night.

During the years of my ministry, I have visited people like these and asked myself what I would feel if I were in their situation. I have also wondered what they think about the plan of God for them. I have learned most from one of my own confreres, another Missionary of the Sacred Heart. He offered me many opportunities to ask both of my questions and to learn the answer about God's plan for his life.

Roger was a priest, now deceased, who suffered from multiple sclerosis for thirty years. In his youth he had been a football player on the varsity squad of his university. After military service as an officer, he decided to study for the priesthood in a religious order. He was still in his thirties and just beginning his ministry when the disease began, with only occasional loss of control of his muscles. It progressed to the point where he could move only his head as he sat, day after day, in a wheelchair.

A man who had been an agile athlete and in control of others as a military officer came to the place where he could not control even his own body. He needed to be fed and clothed, placed in his special wheelchair in the morning, and put to bed at night. He never did learn to read a book by using a pencil in his mouth. Instead, he would pass the hours watching television which someone else had turned on for him. His favorite viewing, of course, was sporting events. He also did much praying.

Before the onset of his illness, he had been active in a preaching band. He truly enjoyed his ministry and believed that he was able to help many people come to a closer relationship with Jesus. The meaning of his call to the priesthood was clear to him. His would be a life of reaching out in Jesus' name to a world very much in need of hearing about Jesus.

The Jesus whom we meet in the Gospels clearly expected his apostles to be, like himself, active messengers of the good news. On one occasion, Jesus told Peter:

> "Let us go on to the neighboring towns, so that I may proclaim the message there also; for that is what I came out to do." And he went throughout Galilee, proclaiming the message in their synagogues and casting out demons (Mk. 1:38-39).

The apostle Paul describes in detail his numerous labors on behalf of the gospel, even in the midst of great adversity. Throughout the history of the Church there have been saints who have continued their ministry even when they were infirm from age or illness. These stories of dedication can make a person who is truly impeded by illness or infirmity feel guilty about not laboring for the gospel. For someone in Roger's situation, the guilt is not rational; yet the feeling was quite real. The deeper the dedication of the apostle to the loving service of the Lord, the more acute the feeling of guilt.

When his illness had brought him to the point where he was beginning to be helpless, Roger became quite depressed. He prayed for a miraculous cure, but none came. He asked, "Why did Jesus draw me to become a priest and then allow this to happen to me? What good is it to be a priest if I can't do the work of a priest?"

In the course of his illness, Roger gradually came to terms with the fact that he was and would always be an invalid. He understood that his ministry as a priest would resemble Jesus' ministry as he hung fixed to a cross. He realized that he was called to let go of all control over his life and abandon himself entirely to the plan of Jesus. He was to imitate Jesus who had abandoned himself to the plan of his Father. Jesus' self-abandonment was a loving obedience responding to his Father's love for him and for those Jesus had come to save. Jesus had invited Roger to be with him in his sacrifice, where he would be his own priestly offering with Jesus.

The example of Roger has had a profound effect in my own spiritual life. It has taught me that the ways of Jesus are far higher and deeper than any ambition I might have. Contemplating Roger's predicament helped me to appreciate the value of abandonment to the will of God shown by Jesus on the cross. Any image of the Lord which sees him only as the active emissary of his Father's love, preaching and healing as he moves purposefully from village to village, does not fully encompass the spirit which moved Jesus. His abandonment to the will of his Father was essential not only to his final redeeming death on the cross; it was essential to the active ministry which preceded it.

I believe that the abandonment of Jesus was more precious in the eyes of his Father than the works which it inspired. Jesus' abandonment was a sign of his great faith in the love and power of the One who sent him. That One was and is able to save the world. The Father was able to raise up the Savior and all who believe in Jesus. Jesus firmly believed this, and so could give himself over entirely into the hands of his Father.

Who is Jesus? He is the "failure" hanging on the cross. He is the victim seemingly without any power even to move his limbs. He is in the suffering of Roger and of all the others who sit in their bungalows, convent rooms or nursing homes turning the pages of a book by using a pencil held in their mouths, or perhaps merely watching television and praying. He is in the lives of those who care for them, too.

The inability to move most of their bodies, which is the trial of those who suffer from multiple sclerosis, is certainly a far more serious disability than the infirmities of age. Yet the limitations imposed by age can generate thoughts and feelings similar to those of people who have MS. Many an old priest or nun or spouse or parent has had to face the helplessness and dependence on others which is the daily burden of those who suffer from MS. They too may wonder whether their lives have any further meaning. They too may wonder whether they have been put aside by the Lord, out of the main stream of his activity in the world, even the world of their own homes. They may pray with the psalmist:

Do not cast me off in the time of old age;
do not forsake me when my strength is spent (Ps. 71:9).

As I grow older and less capable of ministry in the name of the Lord, Roger's infirmity has taught me to let go of control in my own lesser difficulties. It has helped me, I hope, to be a better priest.

In ministering to other old people whose infirmities are more severe, I tell them the story of Roger. I firmly believe that the Lord loved him all the days of his life and that he is now in the embrace of Jesus in paradise. I believe that his apostolate was indeed quite fruitful, perhaps more so than if he had been a great preacher. His love and example have converted many, including me, to a true understanding of what Jesus really wants from all of us.

❦ PRAYER ❦

You promised your disciples that you would be always with them in every adversity, Lord Jesus. You also promised that the way would sometimes be difficult. In the Sermon on the Mount you predicted persecution but also predicted the reward of those who persevere in their faith and give witness to you. At the very beginning of his ministry you foretold to Paul that he would suffer many things for your name's sake.

Most of us will never have to endure the persecution of which you spoke on the Mount of the Beatitudes. Most of us will never undergo the trials which beset Paul in his missionary journeys. Most of us will encounter illness and infirmity. They can be a kind of martyrdom if they are borne with faith and patience. You blessed Roger and others similarly afflicted, though for a long time they may have difficulty understanding their afflictions as a blessing. In the seeming uselessness of their lives, they are close to you in your passion. There has never been a more productive work than that which you undertook on Calvary.

Increase our faith in the midst of life's difficulties so that we may judge them in the light of your eternal truth. Inspire us to see our lives as mainly an opportunity to be and do what you would have us be and do, whether that be action or the endurance of sickness and infirmity. In the meantime, console the spirits of the suffering, as you were consoled by an angel in the Garden of Gethsemane.

Chapter 16: A Loving Listener

When Jesus described the last judgment in the Gospel of Matthew, he predicted that the saints would hear:

> "'Come, you that are blessed by my Father, inherit the kingdom prepared for you from the foundation of the world; for I was...sick and you took care of me, I was in prison and you visited me'" (Mt. 25:34-36).

There are many ways of being sick. At the time Jesus spoke these words, there was little popular understanding of emotional distress as a kind of illness. The discovery of clinical psychology as a scientific discipline was a long way off.

In the modern world we have a much better understanding of the influence of emotions on our health of body and mind. Therefore, ministering to emotional distress deserves to be listed among the works of spiritual mercy which Jesus praised in the Gospel. Those who devote themselves to the healing of emotional wounds are doing what we may reasonably believe Jesus would do if he were walking the earth today. In fact, he is present among us in his disciples. When they are merciful, he is merciful through them. When we see them expressing compassion and guiding troubled souls, we see Jesus in action in our time and place.

Bob Curtis retired from his job as a construction maintenance worker after 40 years of service. He has a wife and four children (three daughters and a son) all born in the 1960's. For twelve years, he attended night school to obtain a bachelor's degree in applied behavioral science. Later, he acquired certification as a substance abuse counselor. When I inquired about his reason for undertaking these training programs, his reply was, "I wanted to be able to do something to help, to reach out to those less fortunate than myself." He sees Jesus as one who heals the wounded minds and souls of troubled people in our modern world, leading them to the spirit of forgiveness which brings peace. He sees himself as an instrument of Jesus' healing power.

He has ministered to the emotional and spiritual needs of a great variety of people. For ten years he participated as a loving listener in a retreat program called *Life's Healing Journey*. At present he is a co-facilitator of another retreat program called *Healing Childhood Hurts*. Bob ascribes his desire to give himself to these ministries to the example of his mother, who made sure that he that he had a good Christian education and who personally urged him and her other children to reach out to others in need.

Loving listeners in *Life's Healing Journey* enable people to explore the hurts which are disrupting their lives and disturbing their relationships with God and other people. The hurts include grieving over the death of a loved one, an abiding resentment within the family, addictions, the remembrance of sexual abuse in childhood, chronic illness of body or mind, guilt over past sins, unhappy marriages, and many other afflictions. *Healing Childhood Hurts* focuses on childhood and its painful memories.

It is especially difficult for people to let go of bitter feelings about those who have hurt them. They need first to admit to themselves that they have a hurt and are bitter. They need to look at the anger which they may have suppressed or misunderstood. In the relatively safe environment of a retreat, they can endure the sadness created by their self-discovery until they can come to some degree of forgiveness of the person or persons who have hurt them. Often the most they will be able to do at the beginning of their healing is to become willing to forgive when they have made more progress.

Bob, and others like him who are their guides, give them an opportunity to bring their feelings into the open and deal with them in the presence of the Lord. Ultimately, it is Jesus who heals. Bob and his coworkers carry on a spiritual ministry rather than merely a psychological intervention. Psychology is important, and many people need professional psychological help. Even these, however, can often receive further benefit from a spiritual intervention. In this work, Bob can only facilitate the work of the Lord. When Bob ministers to suffering people, Jesus is present both in him and in those to whom he reaches out with Jesus' compassionate concern. Bob reflects Jesus, the healer. Those who suffer reflect Jesus in his suffering, described for us in the Gospels.

Bob also carries on a spiritual counseling ministry, one-on-one, where he can guide those with hurts or other spiritual troubles on a longer term than is possible in a retreat. In his retirement years, he has found a way to follow in the footsteps of Jesus, who went about doing good to all in need. The Gospel relates:

> When he saw the crowds, he had compassion for them, because they were harassed and helpless, like sheep without a shepherd. Then he said to his disciples, "The harvest is plentiful, but the laborers are few; therefore ask the Lord of the harvest to send out laborers into his harvest" (Mt. 9:36-38).

Jesus was clearly speaking about those who have an apostolic mission to proclaim the good news. Nevertheless, we can see in his words a broader meaning. Everyone who leads another person out of the darkness of grief, resentment and bitterness into the light of Christ is, in some sense, a messenger of the Lord.

The light of Christ illuminating their minds and hearts brings them to a moment of peace, when they are able to let go of the burden which they have been carrying. This is also a moment of satisfaction for Bob and the other members of the team. They share in the joy of those who have begun to find deliverance. It is the Lord's way of rewarding those who bring his compassionate love to others.

Most of those who engage in the kind of ministry to which Bob has devoted himself do not have his professional preparation. That preparation is useful but not essential. We do not have to possess academic degrees or credentials to practice the works of mercy. Bob Curtis is a model for us all. His main credential is his love for others and his willingness to listen to them as they work their way through their difficulties.

During many years of ministering to people in mental hospitals, general hospitals, and other settings where emotions have a large role in the healing of the whole person, I have come to appreciate the contribution of persons like Bob who put their faith into practice by helping people in distress of mind and heart. As Jesus said, the laborers are few. Nowadays, this is especially true of clergypersons. Consequently, the remedy for the ills of the world cannot depend solely upon their activities. For the most part, it is the laity who have the opportunity to reach out in the name of Jesus among the people in their immediate environment at home, at work and in their communities.

When the laity band together to provide opportunities like *Life's Healing Journey* or *Healing Childhood Hurts*, their ministry becomes much more effective. There is a special power in the community, because Jesus said that he would be in the midst of his community. In this way, Jesus encourages his disciples to form the bonds of love and unity which he considered so important for the success of his mission in the world. However, it also useful and often necessary to reach out individually. Bob Curtis does both. He gives himself entirely to the work of the Lord.

❧ PRAYER ❧

Thank you, Lord Jesus, for inspiring men like Bob Curtis to want to be able to do something to help, to reach out to those less fortunate than themselves. Thank you for the Christian homes in which they have been reared and the spiritual education which they received from their parents.

The laity of your Church are everywhere able to be instruments of your compassionate love in the modern world. There are many more of them than there are ministers or priests. They are the next door neighbors and coworkers of the people who need help. Often, they have gone through the same torment which afflicts those who seek their spiritual counsel.

The prayer of St. Francis aptly describes the spirit of these dedicated disciples: "Lord, make me a channel of thy peace-that where there is hatred, I may bring love-that where there is wrong, I may bring the spirit of forgiveness-that where there is discord, I may bring harmony-that where there is error, I may bring truth-that where there is doubt, I may bring faith-that where there is despair, I may bring hope-that where there are shadows, I may bring light-that where there is sadness, I may bring joy. Lord, grant that I may seek rather to comfort than to be comforted-to understand, than to be understood-to love, than to be loved. For it is by self-forgetting that one finds. It is by forgiving that one is forgiven. It is by dying that one awakens to eternal life. Amen."

This is the face of the living Christ in our troubled world. This is the touch that heals. May all of us, clergy and lay, surrender ourselves to the Lord so that he may work in our hearts and through our love to heal the wounds of the world. The harvest is indeed plentiful. May the Lord of the harvest send out many more laborers into his harvest.

Chapter 17: A Missionary Heart

Jesus' last instruction to his disciples was that they "make disciples of all nations, baptizing them in the name of the Father and of the Son and of the Holy Spirit, and teaching them to obey everything that I have commanded you" (Mt. 28:19-20a). Obviously, this was a commission for his apostles. However, from the beginning of the Church, its members have recognized that every disciple has been sent into the world to bring the good news. Most of us fulfill Jesus' commission for us in our homes, workplaces and local communities. Our proclamation of the good news is generally the reflection of our faith through the way we live and relate to other people.

Sometimes Jesus inspires a disciple to reach out much farther. Clare Martin is a member of a Catholic parish in which I have ministered for many years. She is fifty-four years old and has never married. She is a caretaker for her widowed mother, with whom she lives. Clare is a full-time employee at a data processing center. For about twenty years, Clare has been especially active in her local parish, serving its needs in a variety of ways.

The family in which she was raised was deeply religious, and she received a good Catholic education. From the time of her first communion, she has had a deep devotion to Jesus in the Eucharist. She feels a close personal bond with Jesus and is moved to live in accord with his love.

Her greatest hurt was the death of her father, with whom she was very close, and whose outlook on life greatly influenced her own. Not long after, Clare lost a sister-in-law and then a brother. When she talks about these losses, even now many years later, it is obvious that there is still some pain, though in the midst of her pain she has found spiritual growth. In her own words, "These losses anchored me more to God."

Another great spiritual influence in her life was her visit to the missions of the Missionaries of the Sacred Heart in Papua, New Guinea. There she saw the simple devotion of the people and the compassion of the missionaries. On one occasion, for example, she was moved by the tender care of a burly missionary brother caring for a boy with a leg infection which had reached the bone. She was also impressed by the risks and the hardships which the missionaries endured "to spread the love of Jesus Christ throughout the world."

For personal reasons, Clare did not choose to become a foreign missionary herself. After all, her mother needed her at home. When she asked herself, "To what is Jesus calling me?" she came to understand that she could have a missionary spirit by touching the lives of those around her. She said, "If I touch your heart, you can touch another's heart." In this way, the love of Jesus can be passed on from one person to another. The touch may be a little thing, and the result in particular instances unpredictable. Yet some will be moved to come closer to Jesus

Over the years she has developed a much greater spirit of abandonment to the will of God. In her early years, Clare needed to be in complete control of her own life and the world around her. But through the losses she experienced and the gentle urging of the Holy Spirit, she has learned to let go of control and put everything into the hands of God. She has found that when she does this, she can feel God's love flowing through her, bringing her a great peace and benefit to those to whom she reaches out in Jesus' name.

In addition to her own sense of being called by Jesus to bring him daily into her own world, Clare has long been active in programs which promote the foreign missions of the Missionaries of the Sacred Heart. She gives of her time and of herself to encourage others to support missionaries in the field with their interest, prayers and material support. Every year, she is the master of ceremonies at a dinner-dance which raises funds for missions that are especially poor. It is not uncommon in the developing world for a mission to have many candidates for the ministry and little money to support them during their training. Without help from abroad, these missions could not grow. The efforts of Clare and others like her provide for the support of these missions and the growth of the Church in distant places.

Clare's missionary spirit reflects a tradition as ancient as Christianity. In speaking of the support offered by the Philippians to his own missionary endeavor, St. Paul wrote:

> For even when I was in Thessalonica, you sent me help for my needs more than once. Not that I seek the gift, but I seek the profit that accumulates to your account. I have been paid in full and have more than enough; I am fully satisfied, now that I have received from Epaphroditus the gifts you sent, a fragrant offering, a sacrifice acceptable and pleasing to God (Phil. 4:16-18).

In her many activities on behalf of the work of the Missionaries of the Sacred Heart, Clare helps spread the message which we proclaim everywhere: God's compassionate love shown in the human heart of Jesus reaches out to renew, heal and save everywhere. Many people have a belief which understands God as a supreme being who is remote from our human thoughts and feelings. The missionary who shares his or her faith with these people enables them to discover a God who entered our human condition in Jesus, who was fully human as well as divine.

Her understanding of Jesus emphasizes the universality of his love for human beings. In his eyes, all of us are equal, whatever our race, culture or even ministry. Clare recognizes the special character of Jesus' call to those who are ordained. Yet she also recognizes the value of her own call. It is the whole Church that is sent into the world to proclaim the good news and to extend Jesus' compassion to those in need.

For Clare, Jesus is a gentle shepherd who is concerned with the spiritual feeding of his flock and all their earthly needs. She wants to be part of Jesus' reaching out to those who have not yet heard of him or who need to come to know him better. By supporting foreign missionaries in their total endeavor, she believes that she extends the saving work of Jesus in her time. Hers is a missionary spirit, even though she still lives at home. Her heart is in harmony with the heart of Jesus embracing the modern world. There would be no voice to tell people the good news if it were not for the interest, prayers and support of people like Clare.

In addition to enabling missionaries to proclaim the word, Clare's work for our missions fosters many other activities in distant places: pastoral service, education of young people, medical assistance, and the building up of the local church by educating local men and women for special ministries.

Clare realizes that the mission is her mission, as it is of all Christians, for all together are the Church and the Church is universal. In her own words, "I and the missionaries abroad are all one family." Though I am not aware of any remarkable spiritual deliverance in her history, comparable to that related of Mary Magdalene, Clare calls to mind the words of Luke:

> Soon afterwards he went on through cities and villages, proclaiming and bringing the good news of the kingdom of God. The twelve were with him, as well as some women who had been cured of evil spirits and infirmities: Mary, called Magdalene, from whom seven demons had gone out, and Joanna, the wife of Herod's steward Chuza, and Susanna, and many others, who provided for them out of their resources (Lk. 8:1-3).

It is all too easy for Christians who worship in well-established faith communities to become ingrown. After all, they have received the gospel message and share faith in Christ. Their immediate personal spiritual concerns can easily become the totality of their commitment to Jesus. There is much good in their deep inner spiritual devotion to the Lord. Without it there would be no foundation for anything more. However, personal spiritual growth for a Christian also means being a part of Jesus' mission universal in whatever way the Spirit leads.

Thus, a great benefit for Clare, arising from the fact that she has a missionary heart, is that her participation creates a closer union with the heart of Jesus. Sharing in his mission is also an act of gratitude for Jesus' love to her.

❧ PRAYER ❧

Lord Jesus, give me a heart which is open to all the world. Disturb my complacency and make me concerned about all the people who have not yet heard of you and of what you have done for all humankind. Give me a spirit of generosity which reaches out to the great variety of their needs in the developing world, the foremost of which is the hearing of the good news.

In every age, you inspire devoted disciples to continue the mission you began so long ago. Some travel to distant places. Others provide the means for the ministry of those who have been sent. All are part of your loving outreach. Each of them has a missionary heart.

I pray that I too may have a missionary heart, formed by my contemplation of your missionary heart. It is only when I see you as one who reaches out in every age to every person of every race and culture that I can have the largeness of spirit which a missionary needs. Whether the people you love are white or black or brown or any other color, they are your brothers and sisters and dear to you. May they also be dear to me. Your prophet once said in the name of your Father: "See, I have inscribed you on the palms of my hands..." (Is. 49:16a). May all of your people be inscribed on the palms of my hands.

Thank you for inspiring men and women like Clare to become coworkers with you and the foreign missionaries you have sent into the world. Clare rightly sees the whole body of your Church as the great missionary which extends your saving love throughout the world and in every age. All who are engaged in this endeavor are important to its success. You call some to leave their homes and embrace the hardships and labors of your mission to distant places. You call others to make it possible for them to fulfill your saving will. Thank you for them all.

CHAPTER 18: JESUS IN THE POOR

A rabbi of my acquaintance was once asked by a woman in his congregation how she might come to see God. The rabbi replied that she could see God in the Torah, where God has revealed the Law of God, a law of justice and love. Far better, she could see God by looking into the faces of the poor. A Christian version of this advice is similar. We can see God by contemplating Jesus in the Gospels. He is the Word of God, revealing the justice and love of the Father. However, for Christians as well as Jews, the living face of God is to be found in the poor. Jesus said as much in the Gospel of Matthew when he told his disciples to be merciful:

> "Then the king will say to those at his right hand, 'Come, you that are blessed by my Father, inherit the kingdom prepared for you from the foundation of the world; for I was hungry and you gave me food, I was thirsty and you gave me something to drink, I was a stranger and you welcomed me, I was naked and you gave me clothing, I was sick and you took care of me, I was in prison and you visited me....' And the king will answer them, 'Truly I tell you, just as you did it to one of the least of these who are members of my family, you did it to me'" (Mt. 25:34-36, 40).

Jesus' words are unequivocal. He expects us to find him in one another and to assist one another in our needs. We all have needs which appeal to the compassion of others. However, some of us have greater needs; some of us could not even exist without the compassion of others.

During the 1970's I ministered as a chaplain in two State mental hospitals successively, encountering the poorest of the poor. Not every resident came from a poor family, but many owned little more than the clothes they wore. The hospitals were still crowded at that time, although, under a recently enacted law, the policy was to discharge residents as soon as possible. Some were too ill or too old and infirm to permit them to be discharged. Many others, however, would stay a few weeks or months, be discharged to the city streets and then be readmitted several weeks or months later. We who were on the staff called this "the revolving door."

These poor people could not hold jobs. When they were not in the hospital, they were supported by one or another governmental welfare program, enough to enable them to live in cheap rooms which were sometimes little better than flop houses. Their occupation was to wander the streets in the business district, to the distress of merchants. Some of the resident/vagabonds were indeed quite peculiar in their mode of dress and mannerisms. I have a particular recall of one gaudily dressed transvestite bedecked with cheap jewelry and badly daubed with makeup who liked to hover outside downtown shops. His presence and that of others from the hospital discouraged more respectable citizens from going into the areas of downtown which these poor people frequented. Very few of those to whom I ministered were alcoholics or drug addicts, though the hospitals did have small substance abuse units. Their common problem was that they suffered from severe mental impairment.

There were many other poor people in the towns near the hospitals, but they were less conspicuous. Some of them were working mothers with low-paying jobs, raising their children as best they could without the help of a husband. Some were pensioners, barely existing in small rented apartments, wondering how they would pay for rent, food and medicine all at once. Others were families who still had both parents but also many children, where even two incomes could not keep the family out of debt. None of these poor people hovered around the downtown area favored by the hospital residents when they were in town. None of them attracted attention. Outdoors, they would be seen only as occasional passersby who could be ignored because they were of no great account in the scheme of things.

During those years, I came to know quite well a young woman, whom I will name Susan to protect her identity. I first met her as a practicing drunk who lived with two men who were also practicing drunks. I had encountered all three in my ministry to alcoholics. The pension of one of them and the supplementary social security income of the other two was sufficient to provide enough for necessities, which included plenty to drink. Because they lived in a neighborhood where an empty apartment would invite breaking and entering, they always made sure that at least one of them was not in a detoxification center at any given time. On the face of the matter, there was nothing about Susan which would lead one to believe that she reflected Jesus.

Still, I could sense in all three, including Susan, the potential to be better than they were. Over the years, the pensioner did indeed die drunk. The other two, however, turned their lives around by the grace of God. I hope that my ministry to them contributed to their change of heart. With Susan, the change was especially remarkable. She not only surrendered herself to Jesus, but she reached out with his love to other people who were suffering from disabilities and neglect. She made a career of doing this as a practical nurse. I am convinced that the seed was already there when she was a "fallen woman." Obviously, the image of Jesus in her now is much clearer than it was then. Yet even then there was a tenderness and warmth in her which heralded what was to come. Jesus was always reflected in Susan.

When we meet the poor in daily life, particularly those who show signs of physical or mental illness, we encounter Jesus. When we watch television and gaze on the faces of starving children in the arms of their emaciated mothers, both surrounded by clouds of flies on an African plain, we are contemplating the face of God. It is a face that is, of course, greatly disfigured. Without faith, we will not see beneath the surface. Yet in gazing on these faces, we receive an answer to our central question: "Who is Jesus?"

In his passion, he too was marred beyond human semblance, as Isaiah tells us (Is. 52:13-53:3). The suffering children and their parents display Jesus' passion to the present day world. Similarly, in the wards of state institutions where people dwell in the chains of mental illness, we can readily find the face of God in Jesus' brothers and sisters. Beyond the walls of state institutions, the infirm and homebound reflect Jesus and the divine image in a form which needs faith to perceive it.

A problem for many who try to see Jesus in the poor is that the poor may not seem to have the virtues of Jesus. It isn't that they have more vices than those who are not poor; it is simply that, like other people, they have manifest faults. The poor can be demanding, angry with slight provocation, careless with the alms we give them, and sometimes show little gratitude. That is surely true only of some. Yet those who might otherwise want to help them and then observe these failings may become disinclined to have concern for the poor.

Jesus himself experienced a lack of gratitude. Luke relates:

> On the way to Jerusalem Jesus was going through the region between Samaria and Galilee. As he entered a village, ten lepers approached him. Keeping their distance, they called out, "Jesus, Master, have mercy on us!" When he saw them, he said to them, "Go and show yourselves to the priests." And as they went, they were made clean. Then one of them, when he saw that he was healed, turned back, praising God with a loud voice. He prostrated himself at Jesus' feet and thanked him. And he was a Samaritan. Then Jesus asked, "Were not ten made clean? But the other nine, where are they? Was none of them found to return and give praise to God except this foreigner?" Then he said to him, "Get up and go on your way; your faith has made you well" (Lk. 17:11-19).

Yet Jesus asks us to see him in persons who bear little resemblance to our mental image of the Jesus of the Gospels. We see him as neat and intelligent, gentle and prudent, and generally quite unconcerned about himself. Why can't the poor be "nice" or at least neat people? Why can't they be prudent, as Jesus was and as we are? Why can't all of them be grateful?

When Jesus chose to enter our human condition, he chose to enter it as it is. After all, he came to save sinners, and sinners have defects. He identifies not only with saints but also with people who are quite imperfect. Indeed, the proof is that he identifies with us even though we may sometimes have difficulty being compassionate to the poor.

We can lose our awareness that Jesus lives in our own suffering and poverty if we do not make an effort to see our situation with the eyes of faith. We can learn to see Jesus in ourselves if we reflect on his words in the Gospel of Matthew cited at the beginning of this chapter. It is more than merely comforting that when we are sick, infirm and poor we are close to Jesus in his passion; it is also true. Moreover, when we are close to Jesus in his passion we are close to the Father who sent him.

❧ PRAYER ❧

Show me your face, Lord, in the beggar by the side of the road, in the old invalid confined to a wheelchair and the four walls of his or her home, and in the multitude of starving childish faces which look out at me from the television news. Show me yourself in my own occasional suffering and need.

These images reveal to me who you are because every poor and suffering human being is dear to you as a brother or sister. Thus, you identify with all of us in our distress. You look at me through the eyes of my brothers and sisters who need my love and mercy. Some of them may be far away, but others are close to home. I see an invitation to offer them all practical love in your name.

A psalm says:

> *This poor soul cried, and was heard by the Lord... (Ps. 34:6).*

Your Father heard your cry from the cross. He continues to hear your cry from the lips of all who are crushed and suffer in every place and time. Enable me, Lord, not only to see you in them but to hear their voices and respond with the love which I profess to have for you. Enable me to see you in myself so that I may have the humility to seek your love and compassion in my need.

Chapter 19

In The Footsteps of Merton

As a young man I was impressed by reading Thomas Merton's description of his conversion and decision to become a Trappist monk in *The Seven Storey Mountain*. I formed a highly romantic notion of what the life of a monk must be like. This was a period when I was searching to discover what God wanted me to do with my life. A couple of years earlier, I had been discharged from the army, into which I had been drafted at age 18. I went back to the university on the "G.I. Bill" and, in due course, entered medical school. During my first year, I sensed that medicine was not my calling.

Meanwhile, Merton's writing directed me toward the monastic life. Within a year, I applied to New Melleray Abbey in Iowa and was accepted as a candidate. In fact, my stay there lasted only nine days. I did not appreciate what it meant to be deprived of the comforts to which I had become accustomed outside the monastery. As a city lad, I also found the manual labor in construction of the retreat house and on the farm to be extremely strenuous. I was profoundly disappointed in myself and also confused.

Over the several years that followed, I lived in rooming houses and supported myself with a variety of jobs, all the while continuing to search for my true calling. Eventually, I was to find my vocation as a member of an apostolic religious order and as a priest.

My brief exposure to the monastery taught me a great respect for the men and women who have been called to the contemplative life—and for the life itself. It taught me something about Jesus. He was an apostolic person, and during his lifetime he ministered directly to the needs of thousands of people, particularly the poor. Indeed, that is why his Father sent him into the world. However, he was also a person of deep prayer, particularly before important decisions. Luke tells us:

> Now during those days he went out to the mountain to pray;
> and he spent the night in prayer to God. And when day came,

he called his disciples and chose twelve of them, whom he also named apostles. . . (Lk. 6:12-13).

There were other occasions when the Gospels imply that Jesus simply wanted to pray in solitude. Matthew relates:

Immediately he made the disciples get into the boat and go on ahead to the other side, while he dismissed the crowds. And after he had dismissed the crowds, he went up the mountain by himself to pray. When evening came, he was there alone... (Mt. 14:22-23).

Thus, early in life I was able to see Jesus as a contemplative, a man of prayer.

The atmosphere of the monastery was itself a revelation of Jesus. It did this in two principal ways. First, silent life on a farm close to nature, with silence and labor interrupted only by the chanting of prayers in the chapel, allowed Jesus' voice in nature to be heard throughout the day. His revelation of himself in natural beauty was unhindered in the monastic setting. Even through nature, he revealed himself as a source of peace.

This effect was enhanced by the peace which prevailed among the monks who had chosen to live in a harmony of mutual love and spiritual support. The monastery preached Jesus' peace by its very presence. It spoke of his faithfulness by its enduring consecration to the work of God in prayer and manual labor, century after century. It says to the one who asks, "Who is Jesus?" that he is a living presence waiting for us to quiet our souls and let him enter.

I have since met men who have been able to capture the contemplative spirit of the monastic life, even while they labor in the apostolic ministry. These men come very close to an exact imitation of Jesus. One in particular stands out. I shall call him Father Bryan.

Over fifty years ago he was sent as a missionary to a South Seas island, where he ministered in the "bush" by bringing the local people the sacraments of the Catholic Church, instructing them in the faith and helping build up the infrastructure of his island world. Missionaries in his area often had to play doctor, engineer and mediator, among other secular enterprises, while they were carrying on their religious activities.

I came to know Father Bryan through personal contact when he came to live for some months in my religious community, at the end of his long career in the foreign mission. While he was living here, I came to appreciate his prayer life. At five o'clock in the morning, I could find him in the chapel, deep in prayer. From what others had told me about his prayer habits in the mission and in the United States, I knew that by the time I arrived he had likely been there for some time.

This prayerful old missionary, who delighted in spending time with his Lord, was graced with a great sense of humor. He truly enjoyed life, even in his old age. He reminded me of more than one monk I had met who had the same qualities of cheerfulness coupled with prayerfulness. He was also very much a member of the community, affable and gracious in his manner. His was not a withdrawn, purely private spirituality. I could see Jesus in him.

Men and women of deep prayer, whether monks or nuns or Father Bryan, reflect Jesus to us because they are led by the same Holy Spirit who led the Lord during his earthly ministry. The Gospels tell us that Jesus was consciously guided by the Spirit:

> Then Jesus was led up by the Spirit into the wilderness to be tempted by the devil (Mt. 4:1).
>
> Then Jesus, filled with the power of the Spirit, returned to Galilee, and a report about him spread through all the surrounding country (Lk. 4:14).

The Spirit led Jesus to speak and act entirely in harmony with the mind and will of his Father:

> "If I am not doing the works of my Father, then do not believe me. But if I do them, even though you do not believe me, believe the works, so that you may know and understand that the Father is in me and I am in the Father" (Jn. 10:37-38).

We who have come along 2000 years later cannot be eyewitnesses of Jesus and the power of the Spirit moving him. But we can see his reflection in disciples who have been formed by the same Spirit in our time and place. The monks and nuns who dedicate themselves entirely to the will of God, letting their lives be led by the Holy Spirit to ever closer union with God, show us Jesus at prayer. Father Bryan shows us Jesus at prayer and reaching out with kindness to the flock entrusted to him and to his brother missionaries. Moreover, he shows us Jesus doing so in a thoroughly human way.

My intuition as a young man that I could find Jesus on the mountain with seven stories, of which Merton wrote, was not inaccurate. I could indeed find him there and still do find him in my own times of solitary prayer. Jesus at prayer has always been for me an essential part of my personal response to the question "Who is Jesus?" There is a communication, heart to heart, without which any understanding of Jesus will lack the intimacy which Jesus has desired for all his disciples. Just as Jesus spoke intimately with his Father when he was on the mountain, so too he calls us to speak intimately *with* him, and *through* him with his Father. Then we will be ready to be led by the Holy Spirit in both our prayer and labor on behalf of the gospel. For a monk or nun, the labor will take place mostly within the community of love to which Jesus has called his contemplative brothers and sisters.

However, it was Jesus' will that I also learn to find him along country roads and in the villages where he taught. In doing so, I could then teach others how to listen to him. In the great plan of the Church there needs to be a great variety of expressions of the Lord whom we discover in the Gospels. The Church has needed Thomas Merton and others less famous who live in the solitude of the monastery. It has also needed Father Bryan to show the world the fruits of the contemplation of Jesus in the cheerful and compassionate love of a missionary.

❧ PRAYER ❧

Lord Jesus, you have chosen for me a labyrinthine path in my search for you. Or is it I who have chosen to make my path labyrinthine? My wishful thinking, anxieties and attachments have not been able to discourage you or prevent you from achieving your purpose. It is a great comfort to me to know that you are so great that you can overcome whatever obstacles I place in your way through my ignorance and mistakes.

Sins are a barrier which need my repentance and your forgiveness before I can make progress. Ignorance and simple mistakes, however, are not barriers for you. You have the long view of what we human beings think, say and do. You see the result of your graces from the beginning. Nevertheless, it would be better for me to be less ignorant and to make fewer mistakes. With your help I can grow spiritually and acquire a measure of wisdom.

You have the ability to use even the missteps of your disciples as steps which lead eventually to you. The lessons learned create at least a little humility and, it is to be hoped, much compassion.

Chapter 20: Two Views from India

In the twentieth century there appeared two spiritual leaders in India who have given us perspectives on Jesus. Their lives are marked by differences as well as similarities.

Mahatma Gandhi saw Jesus as a supreme seeker after truth. He firmly believed that the truth would set his people free. He believed that the way of Jesus, striving for a change of heart in those who were oppressors, was the way for him to lead. He believed too that the way to do this was by peaceful means. Gandhi reached these conclusions in spite of the fact that he remained a Hindu and founded his movement on Hindu thought and tradition. However, he was able to see the truth that is revealed in the Gospels regarding Jesus. Gandhi admired Jesus, understanding him as an exemplar of Ghandi's belief that truth is the way to liberation. He also admired Jesus' decision to suffer for the truth and eschew violence.

Mother Teresa of Calcutta, looking out over the streets of the city and their destitute masses, reached the conclusion that the deepest need of people is for love and acceptance. The greatest suffering is to feel unwanted and to be rejected as a human being. To her it was clear that giving bread to the hungry is not enough. She saw that it was imperative to give bread to the hungry with a love that they could feel. For her, Jesus was one who always met people's needs with love, and continues to do so through his disciples.

There are then these two images of the Lord that are compatible but obviously different. St. Paul wrote the Ephesians:

> I pray that you may have the power to comprehend, with all the saints, what is the breadth and length and height and depth, and to know the love of Christ that surpasses knowledge, so that you may be filled with all the fullness of God (Eph. 3:18-19).

It is the same Jesus of the Gospels who inspired both Gandhi and Mother Teresa. We find in the Gospels the description of a world which in important ways resembled the India of Gandhi and Mother Teresa. In both societies, there was a class of people who were at the bottom of the social hierarchy. The shepherds who were called to Bethlehem on the night of Jesus' birth were just one degree above the beggars in Jesus' world. In India, the lowest group were formerly called "untouchables." They were allowed to perform only the most menial and unclean work, which no one else would do. Their mere presence was regarded as a contamination. For example, one of the renowned controversies during Gandhi's liberation of India occurred when untouchables insisted on using a road which passed by a temple.

Just as Jesus drew the shepherds to himself from the very beginning of his mission, so too Gandhi was particularly concerned about the untouchables and other people who belonged to lower castes. Mother Teresa ministered among these same people.

Gandhi also had a larger political purpose, which was reminiscent of ancient Israel. The land in which Jesus carried on his ministry was occupied by the Romans; India was occupied by the British. Gandhi wanted to bring the British to understand the truth that his people should be politically free. Though the Gospels do not indicate that Jesus worked to throw off the shackles of Rome, Gandhi's view of Jesus emphasized that Jesus was a liberator, though in a different sense. In the Gospel of John, we read words of Jesus which link spiritual liberation with truth:

> "If you continue in my word, you are truly my disciples; and
> you will know the truth, and the truth will make you free"
> (Jn. 8:31-32).

It is easy to see how this joining of truth and freedom would appeal to Gandhi, who wanted to achieve freedom from both colonial rule and from an oppressive caste system. Gandhi judged that in his time and place, the political independence of India was the only way to set them free on any level. Gandhi's appeal to truth would not have been effective with Romans. He rightly judged that it would be effective with the British. For Gandhi, the justice of Jesus was paramount, and he sought it with the added dimension of political liberation.

Mother Teresa emphasized the mercy of Jesus. Her vision of her

Lord led her to reach out and touch the untouchables with love. She wanted to heal their spirits while ministering to the needs of their bodies, as Jesus had done again and again as he journeyed through Israel. She spent her life sharing the love of Jesus by feeding the hungry and lifting dying beggars from the street so they could die with dignity. She was not a political revolutionary, as was Gandhi.

What the two had in common was a belief in the dignity of the human person—that all men and women of whatever station in life are equal before God and equally worthy of respect and love. In addition, they both showed a preference for the poor. These attitudes are in full harmony with those of Jesus as he is presented in the Gospels.

Whether, like Gandhi, we labor for justice for the poor or, like Mother Teresa, give ourselves over entirely to works of mercy for the least of his brothers and sisters, we show others how we see Jesus and what he is really like. Moreover, when we live by Jesus' justice and mercy, we can see his reflection in our own souls.

The vision of Christ of Mother Teresa is perennial. In the early centuries following the death and resurrection of the Lord, Christians concluded from their reflection on the Gospels that Jesus wanted them to come together in communities and that they should be concerned about the physical and spiritual needs of the poor. As the centuries passed, there emerged religious orders, living under a special rule of life. Some of these placed a special emphasis on the kind of ministry carried on by Mother Teresa in our day.

Gandhi's vision of Christ needed the background of a society more rigidly stratified by caste than ancient Israel had been. It had had this form for thousands of years before Gandhi appeared and understood Jesus as a messenger of respect and liberty for every human being. It also needed the emergence of nation-states which would exercise colonial domination with a conscience to which Gandhi could appeal.

Though Ghandi did not have the faith of Mother Teresa, he did have an understanding of truths which Jesus proclaimed. As Christians, we can acquire from both Mother Teresa and Ghandi a deeper appreciation of Jesus' teaching.

❧ PRAYER ❧

Lord Jesus, your Spirit has been active in the world from its beginning and will continue to be active until the end of time. Though you are the perfect revelation of your Father, many who are not Christians have been inspired to express the justice and compassion which are at the center of your teaching. The Spirit of Jesus moves where Jesus wills. From age to age, we learn how to follow the lead of the Spirit in new ways and old while the world evolves and presents us with new opportunities.

Thank you for your generosity in giving to many spiritual persons, of whatever belief, a deep appreciation of the value of justice and compassion. It is especially appropriate that we who call ourselves Christians be just and filled with compassion for the poor.

May I, as a Christian, recognize the need for social justice and desire freedom for all people as did Gandhi. He recognized the human dignity of those who were called untouchables and the equal worthiness of Indian culture in a world dominated by Europeans.

May I, as a Christian, also reach out to those who are in great distress of body and spirit, as did Mother Teresa. May my reaching out extend to those who are closest to me and those who are far away.

I pray that I may lose myself in learning how to give to others what they need to live truly human lives and to come to a knowledge of divine love, at least so far as they can see it reflected in me. I, in turn, want to be a reflection of you so that others may come to know you or know you better.

Chapter 21: Jules

In 1824, there was born in the countryside of France a child who would grow up to be the founder of the Missionaries of the Sacred Heart, the order to which I belong. His name was Jules Chevalier. About a quarter century earlier, the French Revolution had overthrown the old political order and had rejected the authority of the Church. Many revolutionaries were atheists. They believed that reason alone would enable them to build an ideal society, that human effort alone could create a perfect world. They saw religion as mere superstition and an enemy to progress.

Not every French man and woman accepted the ideals of the revolution. From the beginning there was opposition. Some wanted a return of the monarchy; others lamented the attacks on the Church and their traditional religious beliefs. In their eyes, the ideals of the revolution had merely led to many horrors.

The century that followed was a time of political ferment, moving back and forth between republican and royal forms of government. Meanwhile, some Catholics who had retained their beliefs tried to find an accommodation with the new order of the world, while others kept their traditional faith and practice. On the whole, however, the prevailing materialism of the new society had a negative effect on both private and public morality.

When Jules was a young seminarian, he was saddened by the spiritual evils of the society of his time and place. It seemed to him that many who had retained their faith were merely nominal believers. What they professed to believe had little effect on their daily lives. When Jules contemplated a world in which people had lost their spiritual bearings, he asked himself what might be done about this. He conceived the idea that the way to stir up religious conscience was to bring people to see Jesus as having a heart full of love for them. He believed the attraction of Jesus' love would stir their hearts better than any other means. Together with a few of his fellow seminarians, he formed an association which anticipated going forth in Jesus' name to heal the spiritual wounds of society.

Several years after Jules was ordained, he was assigned to a parish in an area where few people took their religion seriously. By God's design, one of the former members of his association was appointed with him. Together they laid the groundwork for a religious order dedicated to their ideals, and they began to work for the conversion of the people in their parish region.

However, even in his early years Jules saw his mission as bringing people everywhere to the heart of the one whom he personally dearly loved. For many years, he strove to obtain a foreign mission territory for his small band. Finally, the church in Rome gave them virtually the entire South Pacific as their mission field.

Jules has been called a "man with a mission." Though his mission began in France, it soon extended to the whole world. Jules saw Jesus as a missionary who wanted to reach out to all people in the modern world, even as Jesus had reached out in his own proclaiming of the good news to people all around the Mediterranean area:

> Jesus departed with his disciples to the sea, and a great multitude from Galilee followed him; hearing all that he was doing, they came to him in great numbers from Judea, Jerusalem, Idumea, beyond the Jordan, and the region around Tyre and Sidon (Mk. 3:7-8).

Many of the people mentioned in this passage were pagans and foreigners. Jesus did not neglect his own people, but he was laying the foundation for a Church that would bring the gospel to the whole world, especially following the efforts of the apostle Paul.

Jules adopted Jesus' missionary vision—that all people everywhere be able to hear the good news that humankind had been redeemed by a loving God through Jesus Christ, who has a heart for each of us. The heart of Jesus was the symbol of the humanity of Jesus living among us to save us and raise us up to the Father. Jules realized that everyone wants to be loved. He saw his mission as telling people that they are loved and that their lover asks to be loved in return.

A spirituality centered on the heart of Jesus has many dimensions: We can certainly see Jesus as desiring a personal communion with each disciple—an intimate bond that is unique and arising from a call to a personal spiritual rebirth. Beyond that, Jesus surely wants a community which shares faith, hope and love. Even that, however, does not reach the limits of his desire for his followers. Jesus would have us all be missionaries in some sense, though not all can go to distant places. That was Jules Chevalier's answer to the question "Who is Jesus?"

His vision has profoundly influenced the way in which I see Jesus. Even early in life I began to be aware of the material and spiritual poverty of many people in my local world and farther afield. However, I did not then appreciate the magnitude of the problem or clearly see the connection between the love of Jesus' heart and the healing of the spiritual wounds of the world.

As it happens, it was not ministry in a foreign mission which deepened my understanding. It was daily exposure to the mental and spiritual suffering of people who were afflicted with mental and physical illnesses or addictions during my years as a chaplain and alcoholism counselor. I began to comprehend the depth and breadth of the suffering of the human condition, and the need of human beings everywhere for a spiritual center. When, along the way, I gave retreats or ministered in a parish setting, the experience confirmed my belief that the spiritual needs of people are universal.

Jesus looks at them too and calls persons like Father Chevalier and the members of the order he founded to become channels of his mercy. God once called Isaiah to minister to his people's spiritual ills:

> Then I heard the voice of the Lord saying, "Whom shall I send, and who will go for us?" And I said, "Here am I; send me!" (Is. 6:8).

Father Jules Chevalier heard the voice of Jesus, loudly and clearly, calling him to be a messenger of Jesus' heart inviting all, near and far, to come to him to be enriched by his love. He has handed his mission down to me and others like me. Each Missionary of the Sacred Heart needs to hear the call of the Lord, for the spiritual distress of God's people continues from age to age.

There is a hymn of which I am particularly fond. It was composed by Dan Schutte, S.J. The refrain is:

"Here I am, Lord.
Is it I, Lord?
I have heard you calling in the night.
I will go, Lord,
if you lead me.
I will hold your people in my heart."

Some of us minister in the spirit of Father Chevalier in the land where we have been born among our own people. Others have gone abroad to bring the good news to those who live at a great distance. It is undoubtedly more difficult to be a Missionary of the Sacred Heart in a foreign land than at home. I admire those of my confreres who have made the sacrifice to respond to Jesus' call to far away places. For one reason or another, all of us cannot go to a foreign mission, but we who have received inspiration from Father Chevalier can all have his missionary spirit in sharing Jesus' heart of love.

❦ PRAYER ❦

Lord Jesus, from eternity, your Father contemplated creation with love. From eternity, you were predestined to be the savior of the world, which had turned from its Creator and fallen victim to many grievous evils. When you were born of the Virgin Mary, you heard the call of your Father and gladly answered, "Here am I; send me."

Then, on the mountain in Galilee before your ascension, you said to your apostles:

"All authority in heaven and on earth has been given to me. Go therefore and make disciples of all nations, baptizing them in the name of the Father, and of the Son and of the Holy Spirit, and teaching them to obey everything that I have commanded you. And remember, I am with you always, to the end of the age" (Mt. 28:18-20).

You have called me and my brother Missionaries of the Sacred Heart as your disciples, 2000 years later, to continue the mission which you began and passed on to your Church. I believe that you would have everyone hear the good news. Our task is to proclaim it. The fruitfulness of our endeavor is in your hands. When we speak in your name, you are near, for you have promised to be with your Church in her mission to the end of the age.

We need young men who, like Isaiah of old, will respond to your call and say to you:

"I will go, Lord, if you lead me.

I will hold your people in my heart."

Help us all, from one generation to another, to proclaim everywhere the great love of your heart for all humankind. Help us to bring all people to revere and love you.

Chapter 22: Jesus in Glory

On its face, the theme of Jesus in glory might not seem to fit in with the notion of Jesus in our daily lives. Yet, we believe that Jesus in glory is encountered in our daily lives, though his presence is cloaked in mystery. To discover how this can be so, we need first to reflect on the divine Word, who came to dwell among us with a true human nature.

All things were created in Jesus and for him, and all things will return to the Father through him. We can look upon the universe over all time as a great trajectory of creation, beginning in chaos and culminating in the perfection of all that is. Our God developed nature and human nature, collectively and individually, in accord with the plan which is in his Word, Jesus. This view of Jesus is proclaimed in the book of Revelation, where Jesus said:

> "I am the Alpha and the Omega.... I am the first and the last, and the living one..." (Rev. 1:8, 17-18a).

None of us can accurately picture the present glory of the Lord. What the apostles and saints report in the New Testament of the ascended Christ are visions which, like all visions, merely represent a reality which is far greater than the vision. Does this mean that Jesus in glory is wholly inaccessible to us?

The answer is "no" and the reason is that Jesus' "glory" is more inclusive than the splendor of the Transfiguration or his Easter and post-Easter appearances. At the wedding at Cana, which prefigured his final work as savior, Jesus referred to "my hour." The hour of his glory encompasses all the events of his passion, death and resurrection. Thus, his glory was present in the suffering of Good Friday as well as in the triumph of Easter.

The early Church was convinced that when Jesus was raised, we were raised, and when Jesus went to his Father, we were lifted up with him. They believed that we now reign at the right hand of God. Obviously, our victory is covered over by the vicissitudes of this world.

Our present experience of the glory of the Lord, therefore, is in our lives, especially in our suffering. In us, as in Jesus during his passion, God is in suffering that is borne out of love. When we suffer, we find in the midst of our afflictions a special bond with the one who suffered for us. This is a comfort to believers who are burdened with illness or infirmity, including the infirmity of old age. Now Jesus suffers in us with the glory he once displayed to the world while hanging on a cross.

Beyond this ordinary sharing in Jesus' passion and glory, God is particularly in our suffering when we bear it with love for God and others under persecution for the faith. Jesus said:

> "Blessed are you when people revile you and persecute you and utter all kinds of evil against you falsely on my account. Rejoice and be glad, for your reward is great in heaven..." (Mt. 5:11).

Ultimately, it is God whom people persecute in his prophets. The glory of Jesus shines forth most splendidly in us in our hour of darkness as it shone through him in his hour of darkness.

At the end of time, Jesus will restore all things to the Father through himself. He will create a new heaven and a new earth. The book of Revelation describes the new order of the world in Jesus:

> Then I saw a new heaven and a new earth; for the first heaven and the first earth had passed away, and the sea was no more. And I saw the holy city, the new Jerusalem, coming down out of heaven from God, prepared as a bride adorned for her husband. And I heard a loud voice from the throne, saying, "See, the home of God is among mortals. He will dwell with them as their God; they will be his peoples, and God himself will be with them; he will wipe every tear from their eyes. Death will be no more; mourning and crying and pain will be no more, for the first things have passed away" (Rev. 21:1-4).

This too is certainly part of the answer to the question "Who is Jesus?" He is the Lord of the new Jerusalem. Even now he is the center of history gradually transforming our world into a more civilized and humane community. We see him working through human freedom, and working gradually. The Jesus we discover by meditating on the Gospels and on his action in the world shows him as desiring our cooperation, for our sakes. Being tenders of the garden was the basis of the dignity we received at our creation. We see Jesus continuing the original plan of his Father.

This view of Jesus also shows him as one who would make society a place of justice and peace. He would reform the world at its very foundations.

The glory of Jesus' Church on earth reflects the glory of heaven. We can misunderstand this in a triumphal sense or we can see in the quite imperfect people and institutions of the earthly Church the disfigured image of Jesus in his passion. The prophet Micah, proclaiming the destiny of ancient Israel, spoke words which aptly describe the glory of Jesus in his Church. It is a universal Church—many nations shall come to it. It will be a community which allows itself to be guided by God. It will proclaim peace to the world and work for that peace. It will be a Church which reconciles all of us with God and with one another:

> In days to come
> > the mountain of the Lord's house
> shall be established at the highest of mountains,
> > and shall be raised up above the hills.
> Peoples shall stream to it,
> > and many nations shall come and say:
> "Come, let us go up to the mountain of the Lord,
> > to the house of the God of Jacob;
> that he may teach us his ways
> > and that we may walk in his paths."
> For out of Zion shall go forth instruction,
> > and the word of the Lord from Jerusalem.
> He shall judge between many peoples,
> > and shall arbitrate between strong nations far away;
> they shall beat their swords into plowshares,
> > and their spears into pruning hooks;
> nation shall not lift up sword against nation,
> > neither shall they learn war any more... (Mic. 4:1-3).

Who, then, is Jesus? He is the beginning and the end, the healer of all wounds, a merciful high priest, one like us who lifts us up into his glory to abide with him and with his Father and the Holy Spirit in a life that has no end.

Lord Jesus, as a divine Person, you are the Word in whom your Father created all that is and through whom everything will return to the Father. As the human Jesus, you were chosen from the beginning to be the first-born of many brothers and sisters, including myself. I believe that you would bring us all to a share in the fulfillment which the Father has destined for you.

Your passion, Lord Jesus, is the beginning of your hour of glory. I inquire how your being disfigured, humiliated and crushed can be called glory, until I remember that one of the names of the Holy Spirit is Glory. The glory of the Holy Spirit does not depend upon external appearances. It is the manifestation of God, and God is in the suffering.

We had been alienated from your Father by our sins. We had persecuted the prophets. We had chosen the superficial glory of this world in preference to the will of God. Your Father has reconciled us because of his great love, which has a glory very different from that of this world. In what seems to us darkness, the divine light shines brightly in the wounds that you bore to fulfill your Father's loving will.

When I am sick and infirm, remind me of the truth that God is in the suffering if only I have faith. When I am old and feel useless, let me consider how you were brought to Calvary and your work seemingly left in ruins. When I am tempted to seek glory in this world, may I remember that your glory was and is of a very different kind.

Let me remember too that your purpose in entering our world was not merely to suffer. The glory of your passion and death led to the glory of your resurrection. You strengthened the faith of your apostles by giving them a glimpse of your glory in paradise. You have promised to raise up all of your suffering children who believe in you. After our personal resurrection we shall no longer suffer. Our destiny in the glory of paradise is to share in your eternal joy.

This day my reason for choosing this or that ought to be that it leads me and others closer to you. The question that should be foremost in my mind is:"Lord, from moment to moment, what would you have me be and do?" Union with you in love is the only lasting fulfillment which any of us can have in this world or the next.

I pray that you may be the beginning and the end of all that I do. This can only be by grace. I pray for the grace to be always faithful to your plan for me.

Epilogue

Bartimaeus, sitting beside the road to Jericho, encountered Jesus once and came to believe that he was the answer to his prayers, not only as a blind man but as a human being. Bartimaeus was not a theologian. He would not have known what to make of a portrayal of Jesus which presented him as the Alpha and Omega of all creation. Indeed, he would likely have been confused by the notion that Jesus is both God and human. Though Jesus' compassion was a reflection of the compassion of the Father who sent him, Bartimaeus felt the compassionate human love which reached out to heal him. For the blind beggar, that was the essential Jesus, the one he needed to discover before he became Jesus' disciple.

We have journeyed with Bartimaeus along the paths that Jesus trod in his earthly ministry and through his passion, death and resurrection. We have searched for and encountered Jesus in our own modern world, doing the same works of mercy which had attracted the blind beggar and many others 2000 years ago. We ought to have formed a more comprehensive answer to the question "Who is Jesus?" Yet, even our more comprehensive answer needs to respect the mystery of the God-man.

Practically speaking, it is perhaps enough for us to see what Bartimaeus saw: an exceedingly kind savior, who is able and willing to show us the way to a full life in this world and the next. The complete revelation of the mystery must await another encounter in the next world, to which Jesus will surely lead us if we are willing to be led.

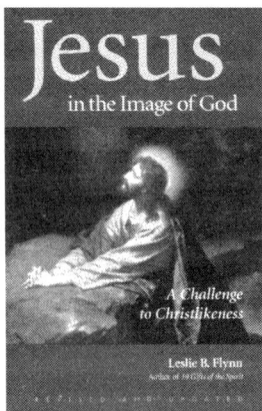